SCANDALS, SIEGES ....

SUFFOLK
GHOSTS & LEGENDS

PAMELA BROOKS

HALSGROVE

First published in Great Britain in 2009

Copyright © Pamela Brooks 2009

British Library Cataloguing-in-Publication Data
A CIP record for this title is available from the British Library

ISBN 978 1 84114 867 0

HALSGROVE
Halsgrove House,
Ryelands Industrial Estate,
Bagley Road, Wellington, Somerset TA21 9PZ
Tel: 01823 653777   Fax: 01823 216796
email: sales@halsgrove.com

Part of the Halsgrove group of companies
Information on all Halsgrove titles is available at: www.halsgrove.com

Printed and bound by Short Run Press Ltd., Exeter

Contents

For Gerard,
Christopher and Chloë,
with all my love

Preface

There are some incredibly beautiful ruins in Suffolk, and there are fascinating human stories behind the stones. Stories of sieges and bloodshed, of visionaries and ghosts, and of scandals among the monks and nuns.

Although there are many more castles and priories in the county than I've included here, not all have legends or tales attached; I've focused on the ones with the most interesting stories, and I've also cheated very slightly by including the Sutton Hoo ship burial and the green children of Woolpit (on the grounds that Woolpit once belonged to the abbey of Bury St Edmunds). I hope you enjoy reading these stories as much as I've enjoyed researching them.

This is also the place where I would like to say thank you. First of all to my husband Gerard and my children Christopher and Chloë, for their enthusiasm in going exploring and visiting all the sites covered in this book (and especially to Gerard for taking over the driving and putting up with my habit of directing him down very narrow lanes, to find a tiny bit of masonry in a distant field). To Dot Lumley, my wonderful agent, as always for her support, encouragement and wisdom. To Simon Butler at Halsgrove, for giving me the chance to tell these stories. And, last but not least, very grateful thanks to Norfolk County Library Service for their help in finding texts.

Pamela Brooks, April 2009

Blythburgh Priory

Blythburgh church. Photograph by author.

The ruins of Blythburgh Priory are not far from Blythburgh church (OS map reference TM 4519 7540), now on private land. They are not open to the public.

The beginnings of the priory

The priory was an Augustine priory; it was founded some time before 1135 as a cell of St Osyth's Priory in Essex, originally for three canons. Up to seven canons lived there at one point, but when the priory was dissolved in 1537 only four canons and the prior lived there.

In 1327 it was said to be the twenty-first richest community in Suffolk.

Bishop Nix's visitation in June 1526 was attended by John Righton, the prior; Thomas Chapet, the sub-prior; and three other canons. They all said that they were satisfied, apart from canon Robert Francis, who complained that the prior was cruel and severe to those he disliked, but lenient to those he favoured.

Dissolution

The priory should have been dissolved in 1528, with its revenues used to set up Cardinal Wolsey's college at Ipswich; however, after his fall from grace, building in Ipswich was halted and the college was shut, and Blythburgh Priory was reprieved until 1537. At dissolution, the priory was very poor; it was worth only £8 (equivalent to about £3,250 in modern terms), including five horses and a cart. The prior was given a pension of £6, but the canons were given nothing.

A turnpike road was built through the village in 1785 and used some of the stone from the old priory.

Nick and Susan Haward, owners of The Priory, found some human bones when they dug up part of their garden, intending to lay a new patio; Channel Four's 'Time Team' did a three-day dig in the area in October 2008, and discovered that the priory was larger than was once thought. Among the finds at the site were a well-preserved skeleton of a man dating from the 13th century, and bones which were radiocarbon-dated to the 10th century – before the Augustinian priory was built, suggesting that there may have been a Saxon church on the site before then.

Blythburgh church and the visit of Black Shuck

Francis Godly printed a pamphlet in London in 1577, entitled 'A Straunge and Terrible Wunder, wrought very late in the Parish Church of Bongay'. It was based on a written account by Abraham Fleming, the rector of St Pancras – who might not ever have actually visited Bungay. A reprint of the pamphlet from 1820 also references Stow's account, which was added to Holinshed's *Chronicles*.

According to Stow, it all started at the parish church of 'Bliborough' (i.e. Blythburgh) on Sunday 4 August 1577, between 9 and 10 in the morning, while the minister was reading the second lesson. Lightning struck through the wall of the church 'into the ground almost a yard deepe' and twenty people who were sitting on that side of the church were flung to the ground. The lightning then went up the wall to the 'veustre' (vestry), broke the door, and then went up the steeple where it tore apart the timber and broke the chimes. And then it 'fled towards Bongie, a towne six miles off'.

The people who'd been hit by the lightning were still on the floor half an hour later; a man aged 'more than fortie yeares' and a fifteen-year-old boy were killed, and the others were scorched.

Black Shuck, in the weather vane in the market place at Bungay.
Photograph by author.

The alleged clawmarks on the door at Blythburgh church. Photograph by author.

However, according to Fleming, the storm started in Bungay and then went to Blythburgh. And in Bungay, it was apparently more than a storm. 'Immediately hereupon, there appeared in a most horrible similitude and likenesse to the congregation there and then present, a dog as they might discerne it, of a black colour; at the sight whereof, togither with the fearful flashes of fire which then were seene, moved such admiration in the mindes of the assemblie, that they thought doomes day was already come.'

The dog then ran down the church; he passed between two people who were praying on their knees and 'wrung the necks of them bothe at one instant clene backward', killing them. He passed by another man and 'gave him such a gripe on the back, that therwith all he was presently drawen together and shrunk up, as it were a peece of leather scorched in a hot fire' – though this man amazingly didn't die.

The report continued that there were claw marks on the door and the stones of the church; and the clock was shattered. During the storm, it was so dark that nobody could see inside the church, except during the flashes of fire.

Afterwards, the dog went to Blythburgh, where it stood on the rood-beam and swung down through the church, where it killed two men and a boy, and burned the hand of another 'among the rest of the company, of whom divers were blasted'; and then 'he flew with wonderful force to no little feare of the assembly, out of the church in a hideous and hellish likeness'.

The Great Fire of Bungay in 1688 did severe damage to the church, burning the original north door, so the clawmarks in Bungay church are no longer visible. However, similar marks – alleged to be clawmarks – were left on the door in Blythburgh.

Was there really a dog? The churchwarden's book and parish register both mention the storm and the fact that two men died in the belfry of St Mary's, but neither mention a dog.

Holinshed's *Chronicles* also mentions the storm, but originally didn't mention the dog. However, the story had already gained currency by 1579, in John Louthes' *Reminiscences.*

Blythburgh church and the death of King Anna

One legend attached to Blythburgh church is that the Saxon king Anna, who was killed in the battle of Bulcamp against the pagan king of Mercia, Penda in 654, was buried there; the black marble slabs near the font are said to mark the spot where he and his son were laid before being taken to Bury St Edmunds. (And in 1763 there was a report that the remains of 500 bodies had been found in a field near the church; they were thought to be the fallen from the battle.)

Another legend has him buried in a wooden Saxon minster, over whose ruins the priory was built; the 'Time Team' dig in 2008 revealed some evidence of Anglo-Saxon settlement, but not conclusive proof of a wooden minster or a shrine.

Blythburgh church and the civil war

There is a story that the church's treasures were hidden in a tomb in the church in 1644 to save them from William Dowsing – who did indeed visit the church on 8 April of that year, and records state that he broke various superstitious images. However, when the tomb was opened in the 1800s, there was no sign of the treasure.

Dowsing is also said to have fired shot into the angels in the roof. However, the kind of shot found in the angels during restoration wasn't used in Dowsing's time. Moreover, there are records showing that the churchwardens paid people to shoot jackdaws that were causing a nuisance in the church, so it's likely that the shot in the angels came from the jackdaw cull.

Another story from the civil war is that local people removed the bells from the church and buried them in Toby's Walks (see below), to stop them being melted down in the Civil War and used to make cannonballs.

The church became badly decayed over the years, but there was a national campaign to repair and restore it in the 1880s. William Morris and the Society for the Preservation of Old Buildings argued that the church should be preserved rather than restored; although they lost the argument, it also meant that the restorations weren't quite as heavy as in other Suffolk churches.

Secret tunnels and healing wells

There's meant to be a secret tunnel running from the priory to Holy Trinity Church; this tunnel may be what's now the vault beneath the Hopton chantry chapel. There's also allegedly a smugglers' tunnel running from the church to the sea.

On the road between Blythburgh and Beccles, there is a 'healing well'; that part of the road is known as Springhole Lane, after the spring that once rose between two stone seats. The antiquarian Claude Morley thought that although the current stonework is from the nineteenth century, the arch was built in 1740 and the pillars in 1280. He believed that it was the place where King Anna was killed in the Battle of Blythburgh (though he actually died at Bulcamp, a bit further west), and a spring rose up to mark the spot; this may be a confusion with the story of Anna's daughter, Withburga, whose body was snatched from its resting place in Dereham and a spring rose up in the spot.

The ghosts of Toby Gill and Ann Blakemore

In 1750, a detachment of the regiment of Fourth Dragoons was based at Blythburgh; their aim was to stop smuggling in the area. Their drummer, Tobias Gill, was known for drinking heavily – he was described as 'a very drunken profligate fellow'. In June 1750, as usual he was drunk and wandering over the heathland when he met Ann Blakemore, a girl from Walberswick.

However, the next morning, Ann's dead body was discovered, about a mile west from Blythburgh, with Toby Gill lying next to her in a stupor. When he was woken, he said he hadn't touched the girl – but local residents pointed the finger. It's possible that some of the local smugglers were trying to get rid of the regiment and used the case to their advantage; but the end result was that the Coroner's Court found him guilty of Ann's murder. The *Ipswich Journal* of 30 June stated: 'Tobias Hill, a black, one of the drummers in Sir Robert Rich's Regiment was committed to Ipswich gaol, the coroners enquiry having found him guilty of the murder of Ann Blakemore of Walberswick.'

Toby was sent to be tried at Bury Assizes in August 1750. But 'Black Tob' discovered that his reputation told against him: a charmer when he was sober, he was a brawler when he was drunk. Most of the local beer-houses had banned him from their premises for fighting.

Although he protested his innocence, he was found guilty of murder. The *Ipswich Journal* reported on 25 August that Toby received the death sentence; he was due to be executed in Ipswich and then 'hanged in chains near the place where he committed the murder' on the following Monday. The judge commented: 'I never before desired a power of executing the legal penalties, but if I had such a power I would exercise it in this case.'

On 14 September, Toby was taken to Blythburgh, still protesting his innocence. Near where the gibbet, was set up, he saw the London mail coach. He begged that a rope should be put round his neck and attached to the coach so he could run for his life rather than being hanged, but his request was denied. The authorities were adamant: Toby was hanged, and his body was left in chains at the cross-ways for months.

Afterwards, the coroner admitted that there were no marks on Ann's body and she could have died from natural causes. So Toby could well have been innocent of the crime. However, the gibbet remained in place for 50 years until it finally fell to pieces; afterwards, it's said that a thatcher used the nails from the wood to make a thatching comb.

Toby's ghost is said to wander the heath in the area where he was hanged; and the smugglers made the most of their opportunity to scare people and keep them indoors at night, and claimed that he was seen driving a coach drawn by four black headless horses. The tale did the trick, and the smugglers continued their work in the main undisturbed.

Ann's ghost, too, has been seen – allegedly she runs in front of cars, and then disappears.

The area is now known as Toby's Walks. The 'walks' part doesn't come from the ghost's tracks, as you might expect: they're simply the Suffolk name for the areas of the heath grazed by sheep.

The Blythburgh Wife-Seller

The *Ipswich Journal* reported on 31 October 1789 that, two days earlier, Samuel Balls put a halter round his wife's neck and sold her to Abraham Rade in Blythburgh for a shilling (equivalent to a rather insulting £5 in modern terms!). The sale was witnessed by M. Bullock, the constable; Robert Sherington, innkeeper at the White Horse; and George Wincop, the village blacksmith.

The Blythburgh Approvers

Richard Quynchard of Blythburgh and Geoffrey Chaloner turned 'approvers' in 1309 – in other words, they were criminals who tried to get a pardon by informing on other people's crimes, a process known as 'appealing'. However, if the appeal failed – or it was obvious they were lying to save themselves – the approvers could be executed. Quynchard and Chaloner were in the gaol at Norwich Castle and claimed that Geoffrey atte Bush of Brampton killed Thomas, son of John Spark of Yelverton, at Trowse on 25 May and stole goods worth 12 pence; they also said he stole cloth and goods worth 8 shillings from two foreigners. Geoffrey atte Bush said he wanted to defend himself in a duel; but Quynchard said he couldn't duel because he'd lost two fingers on his right hand and couldn't hold a sword. So Geoffrey went to court; he was acquitted, and Quynchard and Chaloner were hanged for giving false appeal.

Bungay Castle

Remains of Bungay Castle, showing the old houses between the towers; plate from
Thomas Kitson Cromwell's Excursions Through Suffolk, *1818-9.*
Photograph by author.

B ungay Castle is in the middle of Bungay (OS grid reference TM 335 897); it's
owned by the Bungay Castle Trust and is open to the public.

The beginnings of the castle

After the Norman Conquest, William gave Bungay to William de Noyers, who built
a motte-and-bailey castle, with ditches around the base of the mound and a
wooden fence encircling a timber hall at the top.

In 1103, Henry I bestowed the castle on Roger Bigod, whose family had helped
Henry to seize the throne. Roger spent his time at Framlingham rather than at
Bungay; he died in 1107. Bungay was inherited by William Bigod, Roger's eldest
son; but when William died in 1120 aboard the White Ship (the ship in which Henry
I's son was also travelling; it hit rocks and sank when it tried to overtake the king's
ship in the dark) the estates were inherited by William's younger brother, known
as 'Hugh the Bold' or 'Bigod the Restless'.

Hugh supported King Stephen at first, and told the Archbishop of Canterbury that, on his deathbed, Henry named Stephen as his successor. But then, in 1136, Hugh rebelled against King Stephen and seized the castle at Norwich. Stephen retaliated in 1140 by besieging Hugh at Bungay. Stephen eventually pardoned him and made him the Earl of Norfolk (which included Suffolk).

Hugh then began to build a stone fortification at Bungay. But then it suited him to support Matilda's claim to the throne, and again he fought against Stephen.

Bungay Castle gateway interior. Photograph by author.

However, when Henry II became king in 1154, he took both Framlingham and Bungay from Hugh, although he did allow Hugh to retain the title of the Earl of Norfolk. When Hugh died in 1159, his nephew – also called Hugh – inherited. Four years later, Henry returned the castles to the Bigod family, and Hugh began work on Bungay Castle in 1165. He flattened the motte for a new 90-feet-square keep, which was modelled on the style of Henry's castle at Scarborough. It had entrance steps, a guard room and a dungeon. The 30-metre-high walls – which were 5 metres thick at the base – were the thickest in England, and there was a ditch round them; it was taller than the nearby church of St Mary (although nowadays the walls are only visible to the top of the ground floor). It took nearly ten years to complete the building; and in 1173 Hugh joined Henry II's son, the Earl of Leicester, in a rebellion. They captured the castle at Haughley (see page 83), but Leicester was ambushed near Bury St Edmunds and thrown into prison. Meanwhile, Hugh was in charge of an army of Flemish mercenaries, and besieged Dunwich and Norwich; it was said that the king's law didn't reach into Norfolk or Suffolk.

The story is told in an old ballad: 'King Henry marshalled his merry men all'. It starts with Hugh's absolute defiance:

> Hugh Bigod was Lord of Bungay tower,
> And a merry lord was he;
> So away he rode on his berry-black steed,
> And sung with license and glee:
> 'Were I in my Castle of Bungay,
> Upon the river of Waveney,
> I would ne care for the King of Cockney.'

But Henry wasn't one to surrender. He took control of Norwich and Thetford, and in 1174 his army camped at Syleham, near Diss. He ordered 500 carpenters to make siege engines to use at Bungay, and told the architect of his new castle at Orford, Alnodus of Ipswich, to start destroying Bungay. Alnodus had his men dig a shaft to start undermining the castle, across the south-west corner of the keep.

Bungay Castle interior. Photograph by author.

As the ballad said:

King Henry he marshal'd his merry men all,
And through Suffolk they march'd with speed,
And they marched to Lord Bigod's castle wall,
And knock'd at his gate, I rede;
'Sir Hugh of the castle of Bungay,
Upon the river of Waveney;
Come, doff your cap to the King of Cockney!'
Sir Hughon Bigod, so stout and brave,
in When he heard the King thus say,
He trembled and shook like a May-mawther,
And he wish'd himself away:
'Were I out of my castle of Bungay,
And beyond the river of Waveney,
I would ne care for the King of Cockney.'
Sir Hugh took three score sacks of gold,
And flung them over the wall;
Says, 'Go your ways, in the Devil's name,
Yourself and your merry men all!
But leave me my castle of Bungay,
Upon the river of Waveney,
And I'll pay my shot to the King of Cockney.'

Hugh had to give in and meet with the king at Syleham. The King declared him an outlaw traitor, and said he had to surrender his castles at Bungay, Walton and Framlingham, which were to be destroyed. Hugh managed to save Bungay from being demolished by paying the king a fine of 1,000 marks (£666, 4 shillings – or a little over £350,000 in modern terms) – the 'three score sacks of gold' referred to in the ballad.

The other barons also surrendered, and peace was restored. Hugh went to Syria on a crusade, and died in about in 1178. When Richard I came into the throne in 1189, he allowed Hugh's son Roger to have the castles of Bungay and Framlingham, but fined him another thousand marks. Bungay was ignored in favour of Framlingham, but another Roger Bigod, who became the fifth Earl of Norfolk in 1269, rebuilt the castle. In 1294, Edward I gave him permission to crenellate the walls. He made the keep slightly lower in height and refaced the walls, raised the curtain walls, and built the twin towers of the gatehouse, which was the second largest gatehouse in England. It also had a turning bridge, which lifted up and down by the use of counterweights.

However, Roger also rebelled against the king, and joined with the other barons to make him confirm the rights and privileges of the Magna Carta. He died in 1297, just after the building work had been finished, and his estate went to the Crown.

The castle was abandoned in about 1365, and soon started to fall into decay. It was described as 'old, and ruinous and worth nothing a year', and local people robbed the castle of masonry and built lean-to houses against the walls. In 1766 it was sold to Robert Mickleburgh, a builder, who planned to use it as rubble for building roads; however, he found the process of hacking the masonry with a pick-axe more trouble than it was worth and gave up. In 1792, local solicitor Daniel Bonhote bought it for his wife Elizabeth, who was a writer; she had been born nearby and had fallen in love with the old women. She built a house between the gatehouse towers as a summer home; she also wrote the medieval romance *Bungay Castle*, which was heavily influenced by the novels of Horace Walpole and Ann Radcliffe, and was published in 1796. However, four years later, Daniel Bonhote had left Bungay and sold it back to the Duke of Norfolk. By 1817 the summer house was roofless, and it was demolished in 1841.

Next, the Bungay branch of the Oddfellows bought the ruined castle and the King's Head Hotel next door, and built a meeting hall there. However, they sold it back to the Duke of Norfolk in 1898 for £6,000. The site was used for dances and town events, but was generally neglected until 1934, when Dr Leonard Cane, the town reeve, arranged to lease it from the Duke and raised £500 in a public appeal so the site could be excavated and the building could be restored. Archaeologist and architect Hugh Braun supervised the work and published a report the following year. The walls were repaired further in 1964, and the field opposite the gatehouse – which was part of the original inner bailey – was restored. The Duke of Norfolk gave the site to the Bungay Castle Trust in 1987 along with some money to help preserve it. The castle visitor centre opened to the public in 2000, and at the time of writing a further restoration was taking place.

Bungay Castle gateway. Photograph by author.

Tunnels

There is meant to be a secret tunnel from the castle to nearby Mettingham Castle (see page 121); and another to St Mary's church. However, no sign of these tunnels were found during excavations, so it's likely that the legend arose because of the tunnels made underneath the castle to undermine it in 1174.

The Healing Spring

There was a chalybeate (iron) spring in the grounds of the castle, which were believed to possess medicinal powers. In 1700, Mr King tried to turn Bungay into a spa town, based around the spring, but his scheme failed. The *Ipswich Journal* in October 1861 reported that the castle was in a 'sorry state' and that there was a well in the grounds, 90 feet deep, of which the water was 'strongly impregnated with iron'.

Ghosts

It's said that Hugh Bigod, still angry at being forced to pay that huge fine to Henry II, haunts the place in the form of a black dog – and from this and the visit of Black Shuck in 1577 (see page 7), the legend has evolved that the castle is Black Shuck's headquarters.

Another legend about Hugh Bigod was told by Morley Adams in 1914; according to him, on certain nights every year, the Bigods drove out of the castle in a huge coach. The coach was drawn by four horses, who had flames and smoke pouring from their mouths and noses, and it was driven by a headless coachman who was head rested under his arm. Apparently, the coach travelled from Bungay to Geldeston, past the church, down Lover's Lane, down Bigods' Hill, and then back to Bungay. Morley said that you either see it or hear it – but not both.

Bungay Priory

The beginnings of the priory

The priory in Bungay (OS grid reference TM 3368 8973) was a Benedictine nunnery, founded in 1160 by Roger de Glanville and his wife Gundreda. It was dedicated to the Virgin Mary and the Holy Cross. The nuns built a priory church, which was extended to the present church in the 14th and 15th centuries. Although the townspeople were able to use the church for services, the nuns didn't mix with them; they used the chancel (east) end, while the townspeople used the nave.

Dissolution

The priory never really recovered from the effects of Black Death and was suppressed in 1536. The chapel was turned into a grammar school in 1565. Most of the priory buildings, which were in ruins at this point anyway, were destroyed by fire in 1688. People sought refuge in the church, but it's thought that some brought belongings with them that were already smouldering, and the church was burned out, too. The church was restored and reopened in 1701.

Some of the priory ruins are still visible; in St Mary's Street and Trinity Street you can see the remains of the priory precinct flint walling, and behind the church you can see the ruins of the old priory church – the wall contains a 13th-century doorway.

Bungay St Mary priory ruins. Photograph by author.

Black Shuck

Black Shuck visited the church in 1577 (see page 7 for the full story), but the church was damaged in the 1688 fire, including the original church door with his fearsome claw marks.

Ghosts

There are stories that people have heard women singing plainchant among the ruins, and also the sound of bells that disappeared centuries ago.

H. Rider Haggard – the author of *King Solomon's Mines* – also had a ghostly experience in Bungay; on 9 July 1904 he went to bed as usual, but his wife had to wake him from a bad nightmare. He'd dreamed that he was drowning, and kept seeing the image of his daughter's dog, Bob; the dog apparently tried to talk to him and then communicated that it was dying. When Rider Haggard's wife Mary woke

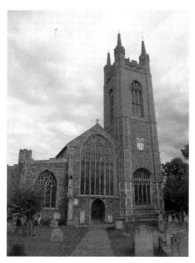

Bungay St Mary priory church.
Photograph by author.

him, she said that he'd been making noises like a dog in distress. The next morning, they realised that Bob was missing, and later that day they discovered that the dog had been struck by a train the previous night. Poor Bob had been killed instantaneously, and the impact had thrown him into the river – all of which tallied with Rider Haggard's dream.

The Druid Stone

There's a stone in the churchyard of St Mary's which is variously known as the Druid Stone, the Devil's Stone and the Giant's Grave.

It's actually a glacial erratic, although there is a theory that it was taken from the ruins of Bungay Castle and used as a headstone. Another theory says that it was used in druid rituals; and yet another says it marks a ley line.

Local legends say that if you dance round it 12 times (or knock on it 12 times) and place your ear against it, you'll hear the answer to your questions. Another is that if you dance round it seven times, the devil will appear.

The Druid Stone in the churchyard at Bungay St Mary. Photograph by author.

Bures St Mary, St Stephen's Chapel

St Stephen's Chapel, Bures St Mary (OS grid reference TL 9177 3443) stands on the site where, according to the 11th-century annals of St Neots, King Edmund was crowned king of the East Angles on Christmas Day in 854/5.

The building is an early 13th-century manorial chapel which belonged to Tanys Manor; it was dedicated to St Stephen. The building was then used as cottages, and finally as a barn; however, in 1931 the chapel was restored. It's usually kept locked but you may be able to get a key from the cottage next door.

St Edmund: the beginning

St Edmund, the patron saint of East Anglia, probably came from the Wuffing line of kings; some sources state that Edmund was the son of Aethelweard. Almost 300 years after Edmund's death, the monkish chronicler Geoffrey of Wells added details of Edmund's parentage and early life to the 'Life of Edmund'. According to Geoffrey, Edmund was the son of Alcmund, a wise, valiant and pious Saxon prince. Apparently Alcmund desperately wanted a large and saintly family; in a dream, an angel told him to go on a pilgrimage to the tombs of the apostles in Rome, and he would have his answer. In Rome, a pious woman saw a brilliant sun on Alcmund's breast with rays spreading to the points of the compass; she said it was a sign that he would have a son whose fame would spread to the four quarters of the globe. On his return home, Alcmund told the story to his wife, Siwara; and Edmund was born a few months later in 841.

King Offa, who ruled the East Angles (as distinct from Offa of Mercia, who built Offa's Dyke), made a pilgrimage to Jerusalem in 853/4. On the way, he visited his cousin Alcmund, and was impressed by Edmund – a tall, fair-haired, handsome lad who had good manners and behaved very piously. Offa had no children, so he asked if he could make Edmund his heir. Edmund agreed, so Offa showed him his coronation ring, saying, 'If I'm far away and I send this ring to you, you must do my wishes without delay.' He declared before the court that he would make Edmund his adopted son and heir.

Offa became ill on his return from Jerusalem and realised that he was dying, so he gathered his council together, gave them his coronation ring, and told them they had to take it to Edmund in Saxony, who would be his successor to rule the East Angles. After the funeral, Offa's men took the ring to Edmund and told him of Offa Offa's request. Edmund – who was still only fourteen at this point – set sail for East Anglia.

The journey was rough and he almost drowned; when he finally landed at Hunstanton in Norfolk, he prayed in thanks for his deliverance, and asked that his arrival would be profitable for his new land and its people. When he mounted his horse, five springs of fresh water sprang up at his feet, and from then on the land had the richest crops in eastern England.

Edmund then journeyed to Offa's court at Attleborough in Norfolk to stake his claim. In November, he went to Winchester to attend the council of King Ethelbert of Wessex, then returned to Attleborough. On Christmas Day, he was proclaimed king of the northern half of the East Angles (i.e. Norfolk) by Humbert, the Bishop of Elmham. He spent the next year at Attleborough, studying the Psalter, and then was crowned the king of all the East Angles at Burna (i.e. Bures) on 25 December 854/5.

St Stephen's Chapel, Bures St Mary. Photograph by author.

The first ten years of Edmund's reign were relatively quiet; he had a reputation for fairness, justice and mercy, and it's said that under his rule a boy could drive a donkey from Lynn to Sudbury, or Thetford to Yarmouth, and no robbers would dare touch him.

St Stephen's Chapel, Bures St Mary. Photograph by author.

Edmund and King Lothbrog

Edmund kept a court at Caister, near Yarmouth; one day, his men brought him an unexpected visitor. Lothbrog, a Danish king, was fond of hawking and one day, when his favourite bird fell into the sea, Lothbrog leapt into a boat to rescue the bird. Whatever happened to the bird is lost to history, but Lothbrog was caught in a storm and his boat ended up in Reedham, Norfolk, at the mouth of the river Yare, where he was found by Edmund's men.

Edmund received him courteously. Lothbrog asked permission to stay and learn more about Saxon ways, and Edmund agreed. Because Edmund shared Lothbrog's love of hawking, he ordered his own falconer, Bern, to accompany Lothbrog whenever Lothbrog wanted to go hunting.

Bern was jealous of the king's new friend; at the first opportunity, he murdered Lothbrog and buried him in a shallow grave. When he returned to the court later that day, Edmund asked where the Danish king was. Bern claimed that Lothbrog had stayed behind in the wood. At that moment, Lothbrog's greyhound appeared; Edmund, thinking that Lothbrog would be nearby, made a fuss of the dog. But when the dog kept disappearing, only returning to be fed, Edmund had the dog followed, and Lothbrog's body was discovered. Edmund soon found out the truth, and commanded that Bern should be put into Lothbrog's boat and cast adrift without any oars or sails, so God would decide his fate.

Somehow the boat made its way to Denmark; Lothbrog's sons, Ubbe, Ivar and Halfdan, recognised the boat. They seized Bern and questioned him. Wanting revenge on Edmund, Bern told them that Edmund had put Lothbrog to death. Lothbrog's sons immediately raised troops of 20,000 men and sailed for England in 864/5 to avenge their father's death. (It's worth noting that Lothbrog's death has also been linked to King Alle in Northumbria – which is where the Danes landed first when they invaded.)

The first advance of the Danes

Ivar carried the Raven standard. It had been woven by his three sisters, who cast magical spells during the weaving so that Ivar would always know the result of a battle; if the bird flapped its wings in the wind, they would win, but if it hung motionless, they would lose.

Edmund defeated the enemy in several battles, but then he was besieged; the siege went on for so long that his men started to starve, and the Danish invaders were also starving. Edmund thought laterally; he ordered a fatted bull to be fed with good wheat, and then be set loose outside. Just as Edmund had planned, the Danes seized the bull and killed it. When they butchered it and discovered that its stomach contained fresh wheat, they thought that the English had plenty of food and could withstand the siege better than they could, so they abandoned the siege – and Edmund was able to save his troops.

The final battles against the Danes

The Danes made their peace with Edmund, and headed north, where they destroyed York and ravaged Northumbria before heading for central England. They captured Nottingham, but Ethelred, his younger brother Alfred (later known as Alfred the Great) and Edmund came to help. The Danes made their peace with the Mercian and Anglian kings and retreated to Northumbria.

But then, in 869/70, the Great Pagan Army marched south again. While Ubbe sacked Ely and Soham, Ivar tackled Thetford. There was a bloody battle, with heavy losses on both Edmund's side and Ivar's side. Ivar sent a message to Edmund, telling him to submit and surrender his lands and treasures, and he could be Ivar's vassal. Although Bishop Humbert counselled him to accept – Ubbe's 10,000 fresh troops had arrived to support Ivar, and no way could Edmund's forces conquer them – Edmund refused to submit to a pagan king.

The *Anglo-Saxon Chronicle*, which was started about 20 years after Edmund's death, says that Edmund was killed on the battlefield at Thetford. However, the more popular account of his death comes from Abbo of Fleury, a monk who wrote an account of Edmund's life at Ramsey Abbey in Cambridgeshire. Although it was written more than 100 years after Edmund's death, Abbo says he heard the story told by Archbishop Dunstan – who, as a very young man, heard it told by a very old man who claimed to be Edmund's armour-bearer in 869/70. Given that there's a strong tradition of telling stories and histories orally, and that people were accustomed to remembering things rather than writing things down at this point, it's a possibility, especially as the dates tally.

According to Abbo, the next part of the tale unfolds at Hegelisdun – associated with Hoxne since 1101 (see page 87), although there is a possibility that the events took place in Bradfield St Clare, near Bury. At Bradfield, there is a field called 'Hellesdon Ley', and within two miles there are Kingshall Farm, Kingshall Street and Kingshall Green. Nearby is Sutton Hall; this is important because Herman of Bury, writing his account a little over 100 years after Abbo, says that the king was first buried at Sutton, near to the place where he was martyred. The site is also close to Thetford – much nearer than Sutton Hoo, the other contender for the first site of Edmund's burial.

The story of Edmund's martyrdom is continued in the chapter on Hoxne (page 87).

The Wormingford Dragon

Wormingford has a tale about a 'dragon' which was actually a crocodile; the story – very much a 'St George and the Dragon' story – is shown in a stained glass window at St Andrew's church.

So the story goes, Richard I returned to England after the siege of Acre with a 'cokadrille', which had been given to him for supporting the claim of Lusignan to

The Bures 'dragon' – stained glass window from St Andrew's Church, Wormingford.
Photograph by author.

the throne of Jerusalem. The beast was described as 'zalowe and rayed aboven and han 4 Feet and short Thyes and grete Nayles or Talouns'. In Germany, Richard was thrown into prison by Leopold, the Duke of Austria, but managed to keep his crocodile with him. When he finally managed to get back to England, he kept the crocodile in a strong cage in the Tower of London, and it's thought that this was the beginning of the famous Tower of London menagerie.

But one day the crocodile, which had grown so large that he managed to smash his cage with his tail, escaped into the Thames. There were proclamations and offers of a reward, but nothing was heard. Meanwhile, the crocodile had made its way up the river Stour to Withermundford (now Wormingford).

The villagers were terrified; they believed it was a monster and thought that they had to give it human sacrifices to subdue it. So they duly fed virgins to the creature, to keep it happy; but then the supply of young women ran out. In desperation, they sent to Sir George of Layer de la Haye, the son of the earl of Boulogne. They explained that they'd tried to kill the monster, but their arrows bounced off its back and they'd run out of virgins to placate it. Sir George came through the forest on horseback, went to the mere and slew the 'dragon'. The villagers of Wormingford never had any more trouble from their dragon.

Bury St Edmunds Abbey

Bury St Edmunds Abbey (OS grid reference TL 857 643) is the remains of a Benedictine abbey built in 1020, with a 14th-century gatehouse.

Gatehouse to the abbey at Bury St Edmunds. Photograph by author.

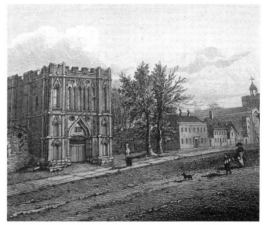

View of the Abbey Gatehouse; plate from Thomas Kitson Cromwell's Excursions Through Suffolk, *1818-9. Photograph by author.*

Ruins of the abbey at Bury St Edmunds. Photograph by author.

Ruins of the abbey at Bury St Edmunds. Photograph by author.

The beginnings of the abbey

It's thought that the first monastery founded at Bury (then known as Beodericsworth) was during the reign of Sigeberht, in about 633. Edmund, the king of England, donated the town to the monastery in 939-46, so it quickly became one of the richest in England. Canute then refounded the monastery in 1020, and the church and many of the buildings were rebuilt between 1081 and 1142. According to the poet John Lydgate, a monk writing at Bury in 1430, some of the stone used to build the abbey came from Caen in Normandy.

The abbey was an enormous place and the writer John Leland described it in the 17th century:

> The sun does not shine on an abbey more famous, whether we regard its endowments, size or magnificence... you would aver the abbey was a town in itself, so many gates has it... some even of bronze, so many towers and a church surpassed by none.

The burial of St Edmund

In about 906, Edmund's remains were moved to the wooden church of St Mary in Beodericsworth; the church was enlarged to make room for the new shrine, and volunteers had to guard the shrine. Allegedly, someone called Oswen opened Edmund's tomb every Holy Week to cut his hair and clip his nails, which continued growing as the saint's body was incorrupt. During the 950s, the Bishop of London came to inspect the saint's body and reported that it was whole, apart from a thin red line showing where his head had been cut off.

During the Danish invasions of 1010, where much of East Anglia was ravaged and Ipswich was sacked, a monk called Ailwin or Egelwin took Edmund's remains to London for safekeeping. Three years later, when the whole of England was under Danish rule and the burning and looting had stopped, Edmund's remains returned to Bury – along the way, miraculously healing the Lord of Stapleford, who gave his manor to Bury as a thanksgiving.

St Edmund's revenge on the Danes

The year after Edmund's body had been returned to Bury, Sweyn Forkbeard (Cnut's father) threatened to sack Bury unless the townsfolk paid a very heavy ransom. Just as he was delivering his speech, he was struck dead. It was probably natural causes – a stroke or heart attack – but it was attributed to Edmund's intervention.

The chronicler William of Malmesbury's version of the legend says that Edmund appeared to Sweyn and 'complained mildly' about the way he was treating the priests; Sweyn was rude to him, and Edmund hit him on the head – and then Sweyn died.

Another version of the story is that Edmund appeared to Sweyn, who was the only one who could see him, and pierced Sweyn with a javelin. Sweyn collapsed and took three days to die, saying that Edmund had killed him.

Sweyn's son Canute certainly believed in the power of St Edmund, because he refounded the monastery at Bury in 1020.

St Edmund's miracles and the missing treasure

Various miracles have been attributed to Edmund – and that included punishing those who tried to misuse him. While his body was in London during the Viking raids, the Bishop of London noticed the richness of the offerings and decided that he should personally look after the saint's shrine. But when he and three assistants tried to take the body from St Gregory's church, they found that the shrine stuck fast and they couldn't move it.

In the 11th century, the abbot of Bury, a monk called Leofstan, wanted the tomb opened so he could see for himself that Edmund's body was incorrupt. As a result, his hands were both paralysed – and he couldn't be cured, even by Baldwin, Edward the Confessor's personal physician. Another version of the tale says that Leofstanus was a nobleman, and when the tomb was opened he was seized by a demon, or had a stroke and died.

A few years later, some thieves decided to rob the church – but Edmund miraculously made them unable to move from their ladders until they were discovered. The thieves were duly executed. As for the woman who decided to pick up coins with her mouth by pretending to kiss the table at the shrine – she found her mouth stuck to the table.

Henry I was caught in a severe storm on the way home to England from meeting Pope Innocent; he saw this as a judgement on his sins, and went straight to Bury, where he made a solemn vow at St Edmund's shrine to amend his behaviour.

Later in the century, Eustace, the son of King Stephen, sacked and burned the abbey's farms when the abbot refused to give him money and provisions to help him fight against Maud. Shortly afterwards, he caught a fever and died at Ipswich – and it was seen as the intervention of Edmund.

Henry VIII is reputedly one of the last victims of Edmund's curse; after he dissolved the monastery, some tales say that he died crying, 'The monks, the monks!'

St Edmund and the missing treasure

St Edmund was allegedly buried in a secret location during the Dissolution, along with a precious gold statue – apparently it was a foot high and represents the archangel Michael. Jocelin de Brakelond described it in his chronicle:

> Above the breast of the martyr, and on the outside of the coffin, there lay a golden angel of the length of a man's foot, having a golden sword in one hand and a standard in the other. And beneath it was a hole in the coffin's cover, where the former guardians of the martyr were wont to put in their hands to touch the holy body.

A. F. Webling wrote a novel, *The Last Abbot*, about the dissolution of the Abbey and the fate of its relics, and apparently used séances to get details – though he couldn't work out where Edmund's body was.

One story says that Edmund's bones were stolen when Prince Louis invaded England in 1216 and were taken to France. St Sernin's church at Toulouse displayed the bones and claimed that Louis gave them the relics in thanks for their hospitality during a siege in 1225. The church was suppressed during the French Revolution and the bones were hidden, but they were eventually replaced in the crypt. However, there's no evidence that Louis ever went to Bury, and there are papal records in 1256 stating that two people should watch over St Edmund's bones. Some of the bones from Toulouse were interred at Arundel in 1901; but, when experts had examined them, they reported that the bones came from several different bodies – some of which were female. So it's highly unlikely that the relics in Toulouse really were Edmund's bones. Plus, given the importance of the abbey, surely its enemies would have capitalised on any idea that the abbey had lost its most famous relic.

So what did happen to Edmund's bones? It's still open to question, though the antiquary and scholar M. R. James believed that the bones didn't ever leave the abbey. So maybe Edmund's bones still lie somewhere beneath the ruins.

King John and the Magna Carta

Although King John signed the Magna Carta at Runnymede in 1215, it had actually been drafted at Bury St Edmunds six months before that. Stephen Langton, the Archbishop of Canterbury, led 25 barons to Bury on St Edmund's Day, 1214, all pretending to be pilgrims.

According to the chronicler Roger of Wendover, the barons gathered in the church of St Edmund; each of them swore in turn on the high altar that if the king wouldn't grant them the liberties they asked for, they would go to war against him and withdraw their allegiance until he confirmed their demands in a charter 'under his own seal'.

The caption reads:

Near this spot
on the 20th November AD 1214
Cardinal Langton & the Barons
swore at St Edmund's altar
that they would obtain from
King John
the ratification of the Magna Charta.
Where the rude buttress totters to its fall,
And ivy mantles o'er the crumbling wall;
When e'en the skilful eye can scarcely trace
The once high altar's lowly resting place –
Let patriotic fancy muse awhile
Amid the ruins of this ancient pile.
Six weary centuries have past away;
Palace and abbey moulder in decay –
Cold death enshrouds the learned & the brave
Langton – Fitz Walter – slumber in the grave,
But still we read in deathless records how
The high-soul'd priest confirm'd the Barons' vow;
And Freedom, unforgetful still recites,
The second birthplace of our native rights.
J. W. Donaldson scripsit, J. Muskett posuit, 1847.

Plaque showing the spot where the barons discussed the Magna Carta at the abbey, Bury St Edmunds. Photograph by author.

Fights with the townsfolk

There were many fights between the townsfolk and the abbey in the 13th and 14th centuries, particularly because the Abbot of Bury St Edmunds had to give permission before any officer of the king could be an official in Bury or hold a court. Unsurprisingly, the tension between the two sides tended to erupt every so often.

The first big flashpoint was in 1264, when some of the men tried to form a guild; they closed the town gates against officials from the abbey, and the abbot appealed to the King. The burgesses had to pay a fine of £40 (equivalent to over £20,000 in modern terms) in compensation. Nearly 30 years later, in 1292, the town was allowed to choose four men to keep the four town gates – but the abbot had the final say over the gatekeepers. Riots followed, and the burgesses wanted their chief official to be called a mayor; however, the abbot thought they were trying to usurp his powers and refused. In 1305, the Abbot claimed that the townspeople had refused to pay tolls due to the abbey, that people had throwing stones to damage the roof of the abbey and then annoyed the workmen who were trying to repair them. The result was a fine for the townspeople. Nine years later, the town was fined £200 when some of the monks who were collecting rents were beaten up.

But matters really came to a head in 1327.

The Great Riot of 1327

Although the townsfolk had persuaded the abbot to agree that the corporation could elect any aldermen, the aldermen had to be confirmed by the abbot and take an oath of allegiance to him.

On 15 January 1327, the king and his army were miles away in Scotland, and the townspeople thought that it was a reasonably safe time for them to attack the abbot and force him to let them have more say in governing their own town. They gathered a force of around 3,000 people from the neighbouring villages and, led by the alderman and chief burgesses, attacked the abbey. They demolished the gates, doors and windows; beat up the monastic servants; and then plundered the abbey. The list of what the abbot said they took was incredible, including: plate; books; vestments; £500 (the equivalent of more than £210,000 in modern terms); 3,000 florins (i.e. another £500); thirteen different charters from Canute, Hardicanute, Edward the Confessor, Henry I and Henry III; twelve papal bulls; deeds; and financial papers. The townspeople burned much of the monastery and its property in and around Bury. They also elected an alderman, John de Berton, without waiting for the abbot's approval; he cancelled all rent and debts due to the abbey.

As the abbot, Richard de Draughton, was attending Parliament in London, they kidnapped the prior, Peter de Clapton, and 12 of the monks, and forced them to sign a deed which said that they owed £10,000 to Oliver Kemp and five other townsmen; the deed also wrote off the townsfolk's debts to the monastery, and gave a promise that the abbey wouldn't to take them to court for damages.

On the abbot's return, he met with de Berton and agreed to all his demands. He said he was going to London to get Crown approval, but actually he appealed against the agreement he'd made with de Berton and the agreement was cancelled. Unsurprisingly, the townspeople were not happy and rioted again; they destroyed the conduits which gave the abbey fresh water, destroyed the church doors of St Mary and St James, and looted the abbey.

The monks weren't completely whiter than white, though, because in the October they attacked some of the townsmen during a church service. But in November the abbey had the upper hand; the Pope excommunicated the townspeople who had been involved in attacking the abbey, and the king sent an army to suppress the disturbance. The alderman and 24 of the burgesses were flung into prison, and 30 carts full of rioters were taken to Norwich. Nineteen of the men were executed; one was pressed to death for refusing to plead; and 32 clergymen were convicted of helping the rioters. It took five years to investigate, and the list of offences included fishing in the monastery's fishponds, mowing the meadows and felling the trees, cutting off the abbey's water supply, taking away 100 horses, 120 oxen, 200 cows, 300 bullocks, 10,000 sheep and 300 pigs, worth £6,000 (the equivalent of more than two and a half million pounds in modern terms).The damages were estimated at an incredible £14,000 (the equivalent of nearly £6 million in modern terms). But the Bishop of Ely was commissioned to look into the affair and he drew up an agreement between the abbey and the townsfolk in the presence of the king, in 1331, where the Abbot agreed to let them off paying the damages and the townsfolk agreed to pay a fine of 2,000 marks (£1,332 and 8 shillings – still the equivalent of over half a million pounds in modern terms) over the next 20 years in instalments of 50 marks.

According to Fox, several of the townsfolk were outlawed, including the alderman de Berton, Mr Herring, 32 priests, 13 women and 138 others. However, some of them were furious and vowed revenge on the abbot – which they got by ambushing him at his manor of Chevington. They tied him up, shaved him, and took him firstly to London and then into Diest in Brabant, where they kept him imprisoned until some of his friends found him and rescued him.

Sir Richard Freysel and the fight with the Bishop of Norwich

The townsfolk of Bury were not the only ones to clash with the abbey. In 1345, there was a row between the Abbot of Bury St Edmunds and the Bishop of Norwich, William Bateman, who said that the abbey was part of the diocese of Norwich and should therefore be inspected by the Bishop of Norwich. The abbey went straight to the king, who ruled in their favour. But when the messenger, Sir Richard Freysel, took the news to Norwich, the Bishop of Norwich promptly excommunicated him. Richard returned to the Chancellor and told him what had happened; the justices ruled that anyone who had published the excommunication should be thrown into prison. As the king was abroad, the justices added that the bishop's property should be seized until the excommunication was revoked and damages were paid to Richard – which, under a charter of Hardicanute, were an incredible £10,000 (the equivalent of around £5 million in modern terms). In September 1347, the archbishop summoned a council at St Paul's, and they agreed a compromise where the Bishop agreed not to submit to the monastery to any visitations, and the Bishop got his property back.

The Rising of 1381

The Rising of 1381 led to more bloodshed. (See page 70 for more background to the Rising of 1381.) Locally, the rebels were led by John Wrawe, a chaplain from Sudbury. John de Cambridge, the prior of the abbey, heard that the rebels were coming to Bury, and fled that night to Mildenhall. Rioters prevented him escaping to Ely by boat, but he managed to find a guide to Newmarket. However, the guide told the rebels where he was; the rebels took him to Mildenhall Heath and beheaded him.

Wrawe and the rebels marched into Bury on 14 June; they sacked the abbey, and also the house of Sir John Cavendish, the chief justice. Cavendish fled but was also killed and beheaded at Mildenhall; and the monk John de Lakenheath, who collected the abbey's manorial fines, was beheaded in Bury market place. Rather gruesomely, the rebels displayed Cavendish's and de Cambridge's head in the market place and made them 'talk' to each other. They also crowned Robert Westbrom as the 'King of Suffolk'; and they made the sub-prior, as acting head of the abbey, signed a charter giving them liberties. Wrawe looted the town and burned land ownership documents.

On 23 June the Earl of Suffolk came to the town with 500 lancers and suppressed the rebellion. Wrawe was surrendered to the earl, and later executed; the town was outlawed (and was one of the few towns not pardoned by the king in December) and was fined 2,000 marks.

Storms, floods and fires

There was a major fire at the abbey in 1150, which destroyed the chapter house, a refectory, dormitory, infirmary and the abbot's lodgings; however, they were rebuilt by the prior.

Rather more serious was the fire of 1198, which was described by the chronicler Jocelyn de Brakelond. According to him, on the night of St Etheldreda, the keepers of the shrine fell asleep with a candle burning, which eventually fell over and set light to the vestments and the wood. The fire was so bad that the ironwork around the shrine was at white heat, but luckily the master of the vestry got up for mattins, saw the fire and raised the alarm. The fire was close to the woodwork of the church, but the monks managed to extinguish it with water and by beating the flames with their hoods. Although the shrine was quite badly damaged, the monks insisted that only a couple of cloths had burnt, and they mended the shrine.

On 27 January 1439, there was a huge storm, which damaged the abbey quite badly; many windows were broken and the bell tower was damaged. Every single light in the abbey complex was extinguished, except for the light which burned permanently in front of the Holy Sacrament – and all the lights were later relit from this lamp. On the 29 May, that same year, there was a huge flood; the water was so deep that a boat could be rowed in the nave of the church.

There was a major fire on 20 January 1464/5, caused by plumbers repairing the roof of the abbey church; the central tower fell and the church was gutted. However, even though the flames licked round the shrine of St Edmund, the shrine itself was unharmed.

Dissolution

By the time of the Reformation, peace reigned between town and gown, and when Legh and Ap Rice arrived in November 1535 they discovered that the abbey gave most of its profits to the poor. They said they could find nothing wrong apart from the fact that the Abbot spent much of his time at his granges rather than at the abbey, was fond of playing dice and didn't preach, so they claimed there was a conspiracy of silence: 'and therby with some other arguments gathered of their examinations formerly I believe and suppose they had confedered and compacted befoure oure comyng, that they shoulde disclose nothynge; and yet it is confessed and proved, that there was here such frequence of women comyn, and reasserting to this monasterie, as to no place more.'

They also described the relics they had found at the abbey: 'the coals upon which St Laurence was broiled, the parings of St Edmund's, nails, the penknife of St. Thomas of Canterbury, with his boots, skulls for curing the head-ache, pieces of the cross, &c. &c.' There were also relics which were meant to be able to produce rain, and others that stopped weeds growing in corn. But the worst of the superstitions, in their view, was that of the white bull – so the legend went, any woman who wanted to get pregnant would go through the ceremony of the white bull.

The bull was provided by the tenant of the manor of Haberdon; it was covered with ribbons and garlands, and was taken to the south gate of the monastery. Next, it was led along Churchgate, Guildhall, and Abbeygate to the west gate in a procession, with the woman next to him and the monks and townsfolk following him. When the procession was over, the bull was taken back to his field, while the woman went to St Edmund's shrine and prayed. As a result, she would become pregnant. Interestingly, the legend said that women who weren't local could have the ceremony performed by a proxy – and on 2 June 1474, according to an old deed, three religious persons from Ghent came and offered a white bull to Edmund's shrine 'for the accomplishment of the longing of a certain noble lady'.

The abbey was the sixth-richest Benedictine monastery in England at this point; and the king's commissioners – Williams, Pollard, Parys, and Smyth – wrote to Cromwell from Bury in 1538, saying:

> We have found a rich shryne [i.e. St Edmund's], which was very comberous to deface. We have taken in the seyd monastery in golde and silver 5,000 marks and above, besyds as well a riche crosse with emerelds, and also dyvers and sundry stones of great value ; and yet we have left the churche, abbott, and convent, very well furneshed with plate of sylver necessary for the same.

The monastery was forced to surrender on 4 November 1539; the surrender was signed by the abbot, John Reeve; the prior, Thomas Ringstede (also known as Thomas Dennis); and 42 of the monks. The prior was given a pension of £30; the sacrist was given £20; and 38 of the monks were given sums from between £6, 13s and 4d and £13, 6s and 8d. The commissioners said that as the Abbot had behaved well and was quite old, he should be given a pension of 500 marks a year and a house – and he was indeed given a pension of £333, 6s 8d (the equivalent of about £140,000 in modern terms). However, he was so upset about the monastery being dissolved that he died just over four months later in a small house in Crown Street, without ever taking any of his pension. He was buried in the chancel of St Mary's Church, but the brass was taken off his grave in 1643, and in 1717 his remains were taken away so someone else could be buried there.

The abbey and its buildings were sold for £413 and used as a building quarry.

Monastic ghosts

In the 1960s, a woman who lived in Cathedral Cottages told her friends at work that she'd seen the figure of a monk in her bedroom; apparently, he sat on the end of her bed. Other people who lived in the cottages said that they too saw the figure.

Cathedral Cottages, Bury St Edmunds. Photograph by author.

Another monk is meant to haunt the Nutshell pub; it's one of the smallest pubs in the UK, though it has plenty of ghosts! Allegedly a small child was murdered in a bedroom on the site, and sometimes comes back; other people have claimed to be able to smell perfume there, even if nobody is wearing it. Hanging from the ceiling, there is a mummified cat; it was found in the wall, similar to the cat that was found in the Mill Hotel in Sudbury (see page 139). Local superstition said that it would be bad luck to touch it or remove it, but the mummified cat disappeared in September

Nutshell pub, Bury St Edmunds.
Photograph by author.

1982. It was returned six weeks later, and it's rumoured that the people who took it had bad luck...

After M. R. James excavated the chapter house in 1903, various people claimed to see the ghosts of monks; interestingly, the monk is described as a brown monk, even though the monks in the abbey were Benedictines and wore black habits. Several sightings of ghostly monks have been recorded around Abbeygate; it's also said that a hooded figure has been seen in the Norman Tower. There are allegedly tunnels leading from the abbey to Buttergate, and ghostly monks have been seen floating along the area.

The murder of the Duke of Gloucester

A Parliament was held at Bury on 10 February 1466/7. Humphrey Plantagenet, the Duke of Gloucester, attended and took lodgings at St Saviour's Hospital. He was arrested there on a charge of a high treason and held under guard; however, he was found dead, a few days later. It's said that he had a premonition he would die there.

Plaque commemorating Humphrey Plantagenet at the ruins of St Saviour's Hospital, Bury St Edmunds. The caption reads:

Humphrey Plantagenet, Dike of Gloucester Son of Henry IV, brother of Henry V, uncle and guardian to Henry VI, Lord Protector of the Realm died within this Hospital of St Saviour's 23 February 1447.

Photograph by author.

Abbeygate, Bury St Edmunds.
Photograph by author.

There were no marks on him, and the official line was that he had died of apoplexy; but many people thought that it was suspicious. There's absolutely no proof one

Ruins of St Saviour's Hospital, Bury St Edmunds. Photograph by author.

way or the other, but rumours persisted that he was murdered by poison; Kitson, writing in the early 19th century, believed that Humphrey was smothered with bolsters.

And who was to blame? It's notable that at the time the Duke of Suffolk was in an apartment at St Saviour's Hospital; and it seemed that popular contemporary option held him to blame. The First Murderer in Shakespeare's *Henry VI Part Two* says, 'Run to my Lord of Suffolk: let him know We have dispatch'd the duke, as he commanded.' And, of course, there's the story of Maude Carew…

Maude Carew and the murder of the Duke of Gloucester

There's meant to be a grey lady who haunts the churchyard of St Mary's; she has been identified as Maude Carew.

So the story goes, Maude was a 15th-century nun who became involved in a conspiracy to murder Humphrey, the Duke of Gloucester, in 1447. Maude had visited France with her father, and on the trip she met Sir Roger Drury of Suffolk; she fell madly in love with him. Some time later, she discovered that he'd become a monk at Bury St Edmunds, so she went to Bury and became a nun, hoping that she would see him. While there, she fell in love with Father Bernard – who was actually Roger, in disguise.

Margaret of Anjou came to the trial of Humphrey at Bury St Edmunds. She

Graveyard of St Mary's Church, Bury St Edmunds. Photograph by author.

requested an audience with Maude, and told her that Father Bernard was Roger; Margaret added that if Humphrey was acquitted, he would take revenge on Roger because Roger was the chief witness at the trial. Maude agreed to kill Humphrey to save Roger's life: her instructions were that she should go through a secret tunnel from the abbey to St

Saviour's hospital and give Humphrey poison. Maude did as she was told and put poison on Humphrey's lips; but then her candle blew out and she got lost in the tunnel. Meanwhile, she accidentally took a fatal dose of the poison herself.

She saw a light and went towards it; coincidentally, it turned out to be Roger's chamber. Maude confessed all to him; he led her back to the abbey church, and cursed her as she died. He later repented and wrote an account of the events and hid it in the abbey. It was found in the 19th century; and every year at 11 p.m. on the anniversary of Humphrey's death, Maude walks through abbey gardens and the churchyard.

Although it's gloriously spooky tale, with plenty of drama, there isn't a huge basis in fact. Humphrey may have been murdered at Bury, but Maude and Father Bernard are completely fictional – they're the characters in the novella *The Secret Disclosed*, written by Margaretta Greene and published in 1861. However, it seems that many local people took it as truth and, on 24 February 1862, a large crowd gathered by the churchyard, expecting to see the ghost. When it didn't appear, they stormed round to the Greene house and threw stones at its windows!

The disappearing fiddler

There's a story in an early 19th-century history of the pubs of Bury that a secret tunnel runs under Angel Hill (which Dickens used in *The Pickwick Papers*), and the entrance is in the cellars of Angel Hotel. When the entrance first appeared, nobody dared enter it – but Jimmy the Fiddler went in and said that he would play his fiddle so that people could hear him above ground and know where he was. At one point in Angel's Hill, the sound vanished, and Jimmy was never seen again; though his dog came out of the tunnel, absolutely terrified. Nobody would set foot inside

Angel Hill, Bury St Edmunds. Photograph by author.

the tunnel to find out what happened to Jimmy, and the tunnel was sealed up again.

The story is very similar to one told about Binham Priory in Norfolk, when a fiddler went into a tunnel with his dog – and then the music stopped… Incidentally, the Binham fiddler's name was also Jimmy, so it's possible that this is an East Anglian legend which is retold and adapted locally. Many 'secret tunnels' connected with the old monastic establishments have turned out to be culverts or drainage channels, when excavated; plus there are known chalk workings in Bury. So it's possible that 'Jimmy the fiddler' went down an old mining tunnel and the roof caved in on him, and his dog managed to escape the falling debris.

The Incorrupt Body

Thomas Cromwell Kitson, in his early 19th-century *Excursions Through Suffolk*, says that John Lydgate was buried in the convent church of the abbey. So was Thomas Beaufort, the son of John of Gaunt and Katharine Swynford; and in 1772 workmen at the church were dealing with the ruins when they discovered 'an oaken case, quite decayed'. Inside the case was a lead coffin, and the embalmed body inside was 'as fresh and natrural as at the time of interment.' Kitson describes it as being in a 'sort of pickle', and the corpse's face was covered with cloth. The nails of his toes and fingers were in good condition, and his hair was brown mixed with grey; it was believed to be Thomas Beaufort's remains. A surgeon examined the body and opened his head and breast, where he found that all internal parts were 'in a state of the highest preservation, retaining their natural appearance; and it is said that even some traces of blood were visible'. The body was incorrupt, but when it was exposed to air it 'soon became offensive'. The labourers took the body from coffin and threw it on a rubbish heap, intending to make money out of the lead, but the body was found and reinterred in an oak coffin.

The Mermaids' Pits

One final tale from Bury is that of the Mermaids' Pits, at nearby Babwell Fen Meadow. These were actually the abbot's private fishponds, but Samuel Tymms, writing in 1859, gives the story that they got the name 'from the story of a love-sick maid, who perished there'. John Gage, writing in 1822, places the pits nearer to Fornham All Saints and associates them with the millers' pools – there were four mills in the parish. One of the most common tales associated with pools is that a girl was betrayed by her lover and drowned herself; whether she simply haunted the pool at Fornham or became a freshwater mermaid is unclear. A correspondent in *Suffolk Notes and Queries* in 1877 said that a well in the village was also supposed to contain a mermaid, and a correspondent to the *Ipswich Journal* in February 1877 said that in 1814, when he lived at Rendlesham, his nursemaid used to tell him not to go near the pond 'lest the mermaid should come and crome [i.e. hook] us in'.

Butley Priory

The gatehouse of Butley Priory (OS grid reference TM 3748 4918) is the remains of the Augustinian priory, which was founded in 1171 and dissolved in 1538. The heraldry dates the building to about 1320, and it's thought to be the earliest dateable building decorated with flushwork. It was excavated in 1933 by Sir John Myres; much of the precinct wall was traced, as well as the priory's wharf on the riverside. Saxon brooches have also been found on the site.

Butley priory gatehouse. Photograph by author.

The beginnings of the priory

The priory for the Black Canons of St Augustine was founded in 1171 by Ranulph de Glanville, a lawyer who became the chief justice of England. He dedicated the priory to the Blessed Virgin. He decided to go on a crusade and went to the Holy Land with Richard I; he was present at the siege of Acre. Before he left, he made his eldest daughter Maud the patron of the priory.

The scandal of the lepers

The priory had charge of a leper hospital at West Somerton in Norfolk. But in the 1290s the lepers attacked his house, and in February 1299 a commission was given to William de Ormesby and William de Sutton to look into the matter. It turned out that the lepers had taken vestments, a chalice, a breviary and a missal – and the spiritual neglect caused by the prior provoked a huge scandal. In October 1300 the crown said that the leper-house would be visited by the chancellor or his deputies to check that the lepers were being kept properly, and any problems had to be rectified. A couple of weeks later, an inquisition was held. They learned that Ralph Glanville had originally granted custody of the hospital to the priory on condition they kept thirteen lepers, plus a chaplain and a clerk who would hold daily services to pray for the souls of Ralph, his father and mother. However, the inquisition discovered that, for the last twenty years, the prior had only maintained four of the lepers and got rid of the chaplain and clerk; and for the last twelve years the prior had cut back on the food and drink for the remaining lepers.

The lepers said that the prior used their revenues to maintain his own house in their precinct and gave fairly lavish hospitality; he also kept many pages, horses and greyhounds, and women were allowed to stay overnight. But even stronger was their claim that he was neglecting their spiritual concerns, and the property they took back from the prior bore out their claim. Because the prior wasn't keeping to the terms of his agreement, the hospital reverted to the king. However, matters clearly didn't improve, because by 1399 the hospital was described as 'desolate' and was regranted to Butley.

Scandals and visitations

Bishop Goldwell visited the priory on 10 July 1494 and examined Thomas Framlingham, the prior, and thirteen canons – one was absent. The findings weren't good: the prior was an over-harsh disciplinarian, and punished people whenever he liked and without the consent of the senior monks. He took their rooms away from the canons for the slightest transgression; and, although they'd given him 13s 4d for the needs of the house, the canons claimed that Framlingham's family and 'gentlefolk' friends visited the house too often 'to its great detriment' and wanted their money back. They also complained that the prior didn't give any accounts; and he didn't have any officials who could act if he was ill, because he kept all the offices to himself. In addition to this, there wasn't a schoolmaster to teach grammar, and utensils from the infirmary were misused. Surprisingly, Bishop Goldwell said that he 'did not find much worthy of reformation'!

Bishop Nix visited in July, 1514, and it seemed that all was well apart from the fact that one of the monks, Reginald Westerfield, had a habit of swearing at the juniors. Thomas Sudbury and another canon said that Westerfield called them 'horesons'; Nix told him to stop using 'opprobrious terms' and told the prior to let two of the canons go to university.

The 1520 visitation showed very minor complaints, dealt with by the bishop's injunctions: that the choirbooks were in bad repair, there wasn't enough food, and the monks tended to chatter instead of observing silence in the refectory, dormitory and cloister.

On 21 June 1532, Nix visited again. This time, there were more complaints from sixteen of the canons. The third prior said that the sick were not provided with a doctor or a surgeon, the books and some of the buildings were in poor repair, and there wasn't enough food, 'with a too great frequency of salt fish'. He added that despite the bishop's orders, the prior still didn't make annual accounts.

The refectorian said that the refectory was too cold in the winter, which made the monks suffer from gout and bad colds (which he called gelidas infirmitates). He added that there wasn't enough food, the sub-prior had taken the pewter cups that were supposed to be used by the sick, and the prior hadn't made any statement of accounts for thirty years.

The food was lambasted by the rest of the canons: the food itself was atrocious, the methods of serving it were unhygienic, and the beer was of poor quality. In addition to that, they complained about the lack of accounts, the lack of provisions for the sick, and the lack of clothes for the novices.

But worst was the cause of fraud: one of the canons, Thomas Woodbridge, went to Norwich and was ordained as a priest – but although the prior didn't give him permission and didn't know about it, Woodbridge gave letters signed by the prior. Under examination, Thomas Ipswich confessed that he'd forged the letters.

Clearly there were other problems, because the bishop ordered that the prior had to provide a schoolmaster to teach the novices and boys 'pricksong' (written rather than improvised music) and grammar. The prior also had to give an annual statement of accounts, repair the buildings, and set up a proper infirmary with enough healthy food, drink and medical help for the sick. The bishop also ordered that the rest of the monks should get the same drink as the prior, and the prior should warn the servants about their insolence. He added that the prior should appoint a sacrist (responsible for the care of the church, the lights in the church and dormitory, and sounding the bells for meals) and a precentor (who directed the church services and singing and kept the liturgical books in good repair), and that the benches in the refectory should have footboards and backs to help lessen the cold. He also said that he'd be back to check on the following Feast of the Purification (i.e. 40 days after Christmas – 2 February) that the reforms had been carried out.

Treason

In 1536, one of the canons was imprisoned for treason (though the full story as to who he was and what he'd done isn't clear). However, the new bishop of Ipswich, Thomas Manning – who had also been elected the prior of Butley in 1528 – let him escape; and in December 1536 Manning was in trouble with Cromwell for letting the treasonous canon go. He sent his servant to Cromwell just after Christmas with two swans, six pheasants and a dozen partridges by way of apology, and said that he hoped to keep the king's favour and not surrender the priory.

In December 1537 Thomas Russhe wrote to Cromwell to say that he'd spoken to William Baron and 'opened to him how he shewed matter against my lord suffragan prior of Butley and me for concealing treason of a canon of Butley. He answered, "I heard such a matter," and no more. I desired the bailiffs to keep him, who say he was of counsel with those who broke the gaol; the gaoler had warned him 20 times from the gaol door.'

Dissolution

However, if the prior (bishop) had held out, it would have meant that all the pensions would have been forfeited. So he and eight of the canons signed the surrender on 1 March 1538 and the priory was dissolved. The household was huge at the time – as well as the twelve canons and two chaplains, there was an under-steward and 12 servants (including a barber); seven poor children who were being taught; three scullions; a slaughterman; two sheep reeves; two horse-keepers; a church clerk; a cooper; five wardens who looked after the boats, ferry and river; a smith; two warreners; three bakers and brewers; two maltsters; a porter; a gardener; six women in the laundry and dairy; twelve husbandmen; five carters; three shepherds; two woodmakers; a swineherd; two plough- and cart-wrights; two men who made candles and kept the fish-house, and two beadsmen. Although the prior wasn't given a direct pension, he was appointed as the warden of Mettingham College and given a grant for life of several large manors. The site of the priory was granted to William Naunton, treasurer of the Duke of Suffolk's household; the gatehouse was converted into a mansion in 1737 by George Wright. According to a report in the *Ipswich Journal* in 1877, at some point a chest of coins was discovered in the wall of the old chapel. Another report, in 1872, says that a stone coffin was dug up in the 1790s but nobody knows who it belonged to; the coffin was still on show in 1872.

The haunted gatehouse

During the 1800s, the gatehouse was used as a vicarage; one of the rooms, called the 'Ghost Room', was sealed off. It's thought that the ghost was the spirit of Robert Brommer or Browner, a prior of Butley. Henry VII had granted him the priory at Snape, but Brommer found himself heavily in debt and couldn't repay the money he owed. On 25 May 1509, he killed himself at Ipswich, and was buried in the churchyard at Butley. But in 1510, John Tostington applied to the Pope for permission to remove the body and reinter it near the north door – a place known as the 'Devil's Portion'. At dawn on 26 September 1510, the body was duly dug up; however, it was buried in the road between the church at Butley and Hausen Street. At that point, the ghost started haunting the gatehouse.

Michael de la Pole and the silver coffin

There's a legend which says that the body of Michael de la Pole, the second Earl of Suffolk (killed at Agincourt in 1415), was buried in the chapel at Butley in a silver coffin. However, there is a wooden effigy to him in Wingfield church (see page 152).

Burrow Hill and the Danish king

About a mile away from the priory site is Burrow Hill; legend has it that a Danish king and his ship lie beneath it with all his treasures.

Before gravel was dug from the hill, excavations were carried out in 1978 which showed a cemetery containing almost 200 burials (all bar two of which were adult males) and iron workings dating from the 8th century.

Campsey Priory

Campsey Priory (OS grid reference TM 3180 5450) is the remains of the priory for Augustinian canonesses, which was founded in 1195 and dissolved in 1536. The only remains are within the present house of 'Ashe Abbey', plus the barn which contains the north and east walls of the refectory. They're on private land and are not open to the public.

The beginnings of the priory

The priory for the canonesses of St Augustine was founded in 1195 by Theobald de Valoines, who gave the lands to his sisters Joan and Agnes so they could build a nunnery; Joan became the first prioress and Agnes succeeded her. They dedicated the priory to the Blessed Virgin.

Fights with Butley

In 1228/9 the nuns had a dispute with the monks of Butley priory over rights to tithes. The Abbot of St Benet at Holme and other papal commissioners ruled in favour of Butley, and the nuns appealed to Rome. It ended up in a mess of excommunications, with both sides protesting; eventually, in June 1230, the original rule was enforced, and the nuns had to give up the small tithes of the church and mill at Dilham to the monks at Butley.

Scandals and visitations

Most of the visitations were fine; in 1526, the precentrix, Margaret Harman, said she'd never known anything that needed correcting in the 35 years she'd been at Campsey, though the books in the choir needed small repairs.

However, the visitation of 1532 was a different matter. Two-thirds of the 18 nuns complained that the prioress, Elizabeth Buttry, was too strict; and also that she was parsimonious. Even Margaret Harman (who was sacrist at the time) said that 'the food was sometimes not wholesome'. Katharine Grome, the precentrix, said that in the previous month they'd been forced to eat a bullock that would have died from disease if it hadn't been killed; others also complained about the meat, and that the cook was sometimes nearly two hours late with their evening meal. The bishop told the prioress to give the nuns a better diet, and make the cook punctual.

Dissolution

The priory was suppressed in 1536. Six stone coffins were dug up near the house in 1842.

Clare Castle

Clare Castle (OS grid reference TL 771 452) is an 11th-century earthwork with ruins of a 13th-century keep and 15th-century stone walls. It is part of Clare Castle Country Park, which is open to the public.

Clare is one of three places in Suffolk known as 'honours' (the other two are Eye and Haughley (see pages 57 and 78 respectively). An 'honour' was basically a group of manors or estates, and the lord of the manor had the right to crenellate his buildings (i.e. make castles).

The beginnings of the castle

The first fortification at Clare was built during Roman times and was called Ebury; the original site was half a mile west of the present castle. It was a border fortress town between the Saxons and the kingdom of the East Angles. It was fortified by the Saxons; during the reign of King Cnut, 1015–35, it was held by Earl Aluric, the son of Withgar, who set up the church of St John the Baptist within the castle precincts.

After the Norman conquest, William the Conqueror gave the site to Richard Fitz Gilbert – the son of Count Gilbert de Brionne, William's cousin – along with 94 lordships in Suffolk and a 75 elsewhere in the country. Richard eventually changed his surname to de Clare (though he was also known as Tonebridge, because he had another settlement at Tunbridge in Kent), and built the castle on the site of the Saxon Castle. the site covered about 20 acres, and 250 people plus several hundred horses lived there.

At Domesday, the settlement at Clare was described as including 600 people and many vineyards. The first Norman castle was a probably mixture of wood and flint. The hill was built up to 105 feet, with a circumference of 218 metres at base, and a diameter of 20 metres at the top. The sides had wooden steps, set at an angle of 45 degrees, and the keep was said to be 9 metres high and 16 metres in circumference.

When Richard died in 1090, he was one of the wealthiest barons in William's council; he left his English estates to his son Gilbert. King Stephen made Gilbert the Earl of Pembroke. Earl Aluric originally set up a college of priests within the castle precincts; in 1090 Gilbert gave the college to the monks of Bec in Normandy, and it became a small Benedictine priory.

Gilbert had quite a chequered career, as he was involved in two rebellions against William Rufus in 1088 and 1095. He and Roger, his brother, were with Prince Henry when William Rufus was killed by an arrow which was fired by Gilbert's steward, William Tyrrell, during a hunting party in the new Forest in 1100. Tyrrell fled immediately and, although there was no proof of any plot, it was said that the de Clares had assassinated William Rufus. Henry went to Winchester, took control of the treasury, and was crowned Henry I three days later; Rufus's body was taken to Winchester and buried without ceremony.

Gilbert died in 1115 and his son Richard inherited the castle. He moved the monks from the castle to Stoke by Clare in 1124, and their church became the castle chapel. Caen stone to rebuild the castle was brought along the river by barge, and stone from the priory was reused. The inner bailey had a curtain wall and four towers: Auditorstower, Constablestower, Oxfordstower, and Maidenstower. It also had three gateways, Crowshouse, Redgate and Derngate. Richard was killed in 1136 and his son Gilbert inherited, becoming the Earl of Hertford in 1141. When he died in 1152, his brother Roger inherited. Roger's son Richard, who inherited Clare in 1173, became the third Earl of Hertford and was a leading figure in the fight of the barons against King John; he helped to draw up the Magna Carta (see page 27).

Gilbert the Red – the sixth Earl of Hertford – inherited Clare in 1262. His youngest brother, Bogo, went into the church; though this had more to do with money than with a sense of religion, because the archbishop of Canterbury said he *'was a ravisher, not rector, of his churches'*. When one of the servants of the archbishop tried to serve a writ on him, Bogo made him eat the letters – and the seals!

Gilbert was one of the leading barons who wanted Henry III to make political reforms. He originally supported Simon de Montfort and was at the Parliament of 1265; however, he fell out with Simon and changed sides to join Prince Edward. He led the Battle of Evesham, where Simon de Montfort was killed, and seized London in 1267, holding it against Henry III. He divorced his first wife, Alice de March, and married Edward I's daughter, Joan of Acre, in 1290. Joan took control of the lands after his death in 1295 and married one of his knights, Ralph de Monthermer. On 29 November 1296, it was recorded that her father, Edward I, stayed at the castle for Christmas. Joan constructed new buildings at Clare Priory and was buried there after her death in 1307; according to the chronicler Capgrave, her grave was opened 52 years later and her body was still incorrupt. Another chronicler, Osbern Bokenham, said that many miracles occurred at her grave, including the cure of toothache, fever and backache.

Gilbert and Joan's son, also called Gilbert, fought at the battle of Bannockburn in 1314 against Robert the Bruce. When he recommended that his soldiers should rest before going to fight the Scots, he was accused of cowardice. This forced him into leading the charge and he was one of the first killed. Because he had no sons, the estate was divided among his three sisters. One of them, Elizabeth, rebuilt and endowed University Hall in Cambridge and renamed it Clare Hall. The surviving curtain wall, called Lady's Walk, was probably named after her. In 1866, a gold cross and chain was found in the walk, with pearls on the cross; when a spring was pressed the cross opened to reveal a piece of wood, which the archaeologists thought was meant to be a piece of the True Cross, and a piece of stone, which they thought was meant to be a piece of the Holy Sepulchre. It was thought that the cross once belonged to the wife of Lionel, the first Duke of Clarence, and was given to Queen Victoria, who allowed it to be displayed at the museum in Bury St Edmunds.

The end of the castle
In the 15th century, the castle passed to the Crown, and quickly fell into decay. The building materials were reused locally.

The coming of the railway
In 1863, the Great Eastern Railway built the station and the lines; the construction meant that they had to remove buildings and ditches with moats. The Royal Archaeological Institute was unimpressed, and reported in the *Ipswich Journal* of 24 July 1869:

> With characteristic "Limited Liability" taste, the Railway has ploughed up and passed right through the midst of these charming old ruins…this was done in spite of entreaty, and also despite an arrangement verbally agreed to between the owner, the Rev. W. S. Jenner and the Directors or contractors. A good shed has squatted itself uglily down into the middle of

Remains of the wall by the mound at Clare Castle. Photograph by author.

the ruins! Rarely, even in this age of Vandalism, has the triumph of money bags been more complete!

The country park

Tony de Fonblanque, who owned 14 acres of the original castle site, created Clare Castle Country Park in 1972 and donated it to the West Suffolk County Council; the park is Suffolk's oldest public country park.

Remains of the castle wall at the top of the mound, Clare. Photograph by author.

Ghosts

Strangely, no ghosts are recorded at the castle. The nearby Bell Hotel, however, is reputed to be haunted. One of the ghosts is a highwayman who wasn't pleased about the 18th-century stables being converted to bedrooms, and showed his annoyance by occasionally haunting them.

Clare Priory

Clare Priory (OS grid reference TL 7700 4500) was founded in 1248/9, by Richard de Clare, the Earl of Gloucester; it was the first Augustinian priory in England.

The priory was dissolved in 1538, when it became a private house; it was converted by Sir Thomas Barnardiston in 1604. The house is timber-framed and plastered with a 14th-century stone front to the west.

Later it was owned by a lawyer, Mr Poulter, who had a reputation for being ruthless and terrifying; he was eventually struck off for issuing false writs, and changing names and dates on legal documents.

After that, the building was bought by the Barker family. It was used as a school from 1862 onwards but, although it was well regarded, the number of pupils declined, and the school was forced to close in the mid 1880s.

The Army occupied the priory during the Second World War as its headquarters; after the war, it became a nursing home.

Lady May, who died in 1945, told her daughters that her dearest wish was for the building to become a priory again. In 1953, her wish came true; her daughters, wanting to follow their mother's wishes, sold it to the Augustinian friars for well under the market value of the building so that they'd be able to turn it back into a priory and a place of retreat.

Clare Priory. Photograph by author.

Scandals

Two of the canons from the house – Nicholas Bacon and John Oxeford – took part in the Uprising of 1381.

Just before the Reformation, friar Robert Topley left to get married. He was brought back and imprisoned for being apostate (i.e. leaving the religious life for a secular one without permission), but managed to escape back to his wife.

Remains of the old priory at Clare. Photograph by author.

The Legend of Clare

The legend of Clare was written down by Lady Barker, the owner of the priory, in 1902. She heard the tale from the man who did the carving in the library, who in turn had heard it from an old woman in the town. Lady Barker went to visit the old woman, who couldn't read or write, but who said she'd heard the story passed down through generations. Although the story didn't seem to fit with the layout of the building as Lady Barker knew it, when the priory was excavated years later it was discovered that the original layout tallied with the details of the old lady's story.

Some time during the 1450s, Hugh the Sacristan borrowed money using the priory treasures as surety. He was desperate to find the money to repay his debts because he was afraid that the prior would find out – and also because he was worried that a messenger from the Pope, who was visiting nearby Bury St Edmunds, would come and visit the priory and ask to inspect the treasures.

One day, several of the monks went fishing in the River Stour. Hugh went with them, but stayed behind when they returned to the priory, trying to think of a way out of his problem. A stranger, dressed in a monk's habit, came up to chat with him, saying that he could see Hugh looked worried. Hugh confided in him, and the stranger said that when he'd been sacristan, he'd found it necessary to borrow money short term every once in a while. He then suggested two ways that Hugh could make money. Firstly, he should hide his stock of candles and claim that they'd been eaten by mice; then he could sell the original candles and use the money. Secondly, he could sell votive candles and then, as soon as the worshipper had left, reclaim the candle, trim the wick and sell it over again. The only condition was that he had to keep the first candle. If it ever burned down, the stranger would claim him for ever.

Hugh, who was panicking, didn't think that there was anything strange about the stranger's offer – so he agreed to the deal. He went back to the priory and into the church; at first he thought that someone was following him, and he heard strange clanking noises behind him, but when he reached the high altar he realised that he was alone and shrugged off his uneasiness. He prepared the candles as usual for the midnight service, then went into the sacristy and hid the remaining candles. As the stranger had suggested, he claimed that mice had eaten the candles; the plan worked, as did the reselling of votive candles.

But then some of Hugh's other mismanagement of priory affairs were discovered; he was put on a diet of bread and water and wasn't allowed to go outside the priory. Late one afternoon, he remembered that he needed some salt for the kitchen. He took a candle, fetched the salt and went to the kitchen. There was a cooked chicken sitting on the table, and Hugh was hungry – he couldn't resist it. He scoffed the lot – and then he heard the rest of the monks returning from their day's hunting. Panicking that he would be caught with the carcass, he ran off, leaving the candle burning. The prior was furious when he saw that Hugh had eaten their dinner, and cursed the sacristan.

Just at that moment, the candle burned out and they heard a terrifying scream.

They rushed towards the sound, and discovered Hugh's dead body at the foot of the stairs. His face was filled with terror, and his skin looked as if it had been burned in a fire. There was also a strong smell of sulphur in the air and they heard a metallic clanking.

It seemed that Hugh had chosen the wrong candle – he'd picked the one that he was supposed to never let go out. And, so the story went, the monks could never scrub away the bloodstain on the stairs, even with holy water.

The knights who broke sanctuary

In 1385, the knight Thomas de Mortimer was sentenced to penitence at Clare Priory by the Bishop of London, instead of being excommunicated, for breaking the law of sanctuary.

John de Quintone had stolen some goods from de Mortimer, and had fled to the church at Clare Priory for sanctuary – at the time, any church or parish could grant sanctuary to criminals or those seeking protection. Sanctuary lasted for up to 40 days, and during that time the alleged criminal could ask to see a coroner in the church, confess to any crime, and then 'abjure the realm' (i.e. take voluntary exile).

De Mortimer and six of his followers – John de Nuport, Thomas Marrishall, Griffith ap Llewlyn, Matthew Maybrook, John Mull, and Simon Domvill – dragged de Quintone out of the church, ignoring the rules of sanctuary, and cut off his ears before throwing him back into the church.

De Mortimer and his followers begged the bishop for absolution. The bishop said that de Mortimer had to walk barefoot and bareheaded to Clare Priory, carrying a cloth of gold worth £3 (equivalent to about £1,300 in modern terms) and a candle weighing 3 lbs; his followers also had to walk there bareheaded and barefoot, each carrying a candle weighing 1lb.

Dodnash Priory

Dodnash Priory (OS grid reference TM 1048 3568) was an Augustinian priory founded circa 1188. Although some sources believe that it was founded by Baldwin de Toeni and his mother Alda, historian Christopher Harper-Bill says that it was actually founded by Wimer the Chaplain, who was sheriff of Norfolk and Suffolk in 1170 and bought the land from de Toeni.

The priory was probably meant for between four and five canons; five canons were living there in 1381. The Earls of Norfolk were patrons from about 1272 until dissolution.

The priory was dissolved in 1525, valued at £42, 18s and 8d. Prior Thomas resigned, and the endowments of the priory were intended to be used for Wolsey's college in Ipswich. After Wolsey fell from grace and his college was closed, the site of Dodnash Priory was assigned to Lionel Tolemache.

There is only one lump of stone remaining from the priory, although some reused medieval stone can be seen in Dodnash Priory Farm.

Secret tunnels and hidden treasure

There's a legend that a secret tunnel runs between Dodnash Priory and 'the nunnery' (Bentley Old Hall).

It's also said that, if you can lift the single surviving lump of the priory stone, you'll find treasure beneath it. So far, nobody's been able to lift the stone...

Dunwich Castle

Dunwich Castle began life as a Roman signal station called Donmoc, slightly smaller than the fortress of Burgh Castle. It's also said that a castle was built at Dunwich for Sigebert, the King of East Anglia, as the principal seat of his government; Sigebert died in 637. (However, there is also a school of thought that Donmoc was at Walton, near Felixstowe – see page 67.)

During the reign of Edward the Confessor, the manor was held by Robert Malet. In the Domesday book in 1086, the survey said that the town had three churches and 236 Burgesses. The town was held by Gilbert the Blond, and 80 of Robert Malet's from Eye Castle garrisoned the castle. When Malet was banished, his estates were taken over by the Crown. Henry I returned them to Malet in 1100, but then they fell out again and Henry granted Dunwich Castle to Hugh le Despenser in 1106.

We know that castle was a motte and bailey castle, built within the remains of the old Roman fort; the building was probably started by William Malet to help protect the town from Danish invaders.

Hugh Bigod and Robert, the Earl of Leicester, attacked the town and castle in 1173 during their rebellion against Henry II (see page 67), but failed to capture it. The Earl said that he would be friendly to Dunwich townsfolk, but if they refused to join him they would lose their heads. He put up a gallows to show that he meant his words – but the men and women of Dunwich were having none of it! They prepared to defend the town and carried stones to the fence ready to hurl them at the enemy. Robert and Hugh decided that discretion was the better part of valour and withdrew their 3,000 Flemish mercenaries. Perhaps as a reward for the townsfolk's bravery, Dunwich was granted a royal charter in 1199.

After the castle at Orford was built (see page 123), the castle at Dunwich was allowed to fall into disrepair. However, the North Sea has encroached very badly upon Dunwich over the years, and any remains of the castle are buried beneath thick layers of silt in the North Sea. Because sand particles in the water make visibility extremely difficult, the only way that the exact site of the castle will be discovered is through acoustic imaging technology – such as that used to explore the sea bed in a recent project by marine archaeologists Stuart Bacon and Professor David Sear from the University of Southampton.

Dunwich Friaries

O ne and a half millennia ago, Dunwich was the capital of East Anglia and was one of the largest ports in the east of England. At Domesday, there were three churches, two chapels, a priory, two friaries, a church of the Knights Templar and a castle, and by 1086 there were as many as 3,000 people in the town. More churches were built during the town's most prosperous period, the 12th and early 13th centuries. Dunwich was also important as a shipping community; it is recorded in 1205 that there were five Royal Galleons in Dunwich, as many as there were in the Port of London, and in 1242 when the truce between King John and the King of France broke down, Dunwich was able to muster 80 ships to help him.

However, Dunwich has been very badly battered by the North Sea; the castle (see page 51) has gone, along with most of the churches, and only ruins of one of the priories still survives.

Storms, floods and bitter rivalry

Even in Dunwich's heyday, there was a problem with longshore drift. In 1221, Henry III granted £200 towards the cost of making sea defences.

There was a massive sea surge in March 1286, which eroded a strip of land on the eastern side of the town, up to 100 metres wide in places, and carried away houses and some of the monastic buildings. Then a particularly bad storm on 14 January 1328 blocked off the harbour and wiped out the two 'Domesday' churches of St Bartholomew and St Michael. After the harbour was ruined, the marine traffic went to the port of Walberswick instead of Dunwich. This really hit the town's prosperity, and work on the town's sea walls practically ceased.

The rivalry between the two towns – which had already resulted in bloodshed and court cases – grew even worse. In 1331 a commission investigated claims that four men of Dunwich had attacked a ship belonging to widow Anastasia Butt from Walberswick, murdered the 16 sailors on board and sunk the ship.

Another storm in 1347 wiped out 400 houses and shops; the churches of St Martin and St Leonard were also lost some time during the century. The church of St Nicholas was abandoned in1352 because it was so close to the sea; it became derelict, and finally fell over the cliff towards the end of the century. In 1510, the churchwardens raised funds to build a breakwater to protect the church of St John the Baptist – the main church of the town, in the market place – from the sea, and a further attempt was made in 1542; however, it failed, and the townspeople ended up demolishing the church to pieces and reusing the building materials. During the demolition, historian Thomas Gardiner recorded a stone was removed from a grave and 'two chalices of course [sic] metal' were found on his breast, so it may be that St John's was built on the site of the original Saxon cathedral.

The church of St Peter was the next to be threatened. William Dowsing visited it in 1644 and gave his usual orders to destroy what he called superstitious images, but it was a fairly pointless exercise because the church itself didn't last much longer; it started to fall off the cliff in 1688. The bells and the lead from the roof were rescued and taken to All Saints' church, and the tower of St Peter's church had been taken by the sea by the end of the century.

There was a huge storm in December 1740 which did even more damage – the Cock and Hen Hills, which were 40 feet tall, the previous summer, were flattened. St Nicholas's churchyard vanished; and skeletal remains were washed up on the beach

The remaining church, All Saints, fell into decay and was abandoned after the new church of St James was built in 1832. And even All Saints – which was 149 feet long, hardly a tiny church – was taken by the sea between February 1904 and November 1919. A single buttress was rescued and reset in the churchyard of St James.

Dunwich Priory

William the Conqueror gave the churches of Dunwich to the monastery of Eye. There was a small priory belonging to Eye monastery in the town, but it was engulfed by the sea in 1286. The 'Red Book of Eye', which had belonged to St Felix, was brought to the monastery of Eye from Dunwich Priory. The last traces of the priory were written about shortly after they were washed away in 1740; it seemed that Covent Garden, next to Sea Field, was formerly the garden of the priory. Thyme was grown on it as a crop but, when the sea encroached on it, many human remains were discovered and it was thought that the garden was actually a former graveyard of the priory.

The Dominican (Blackfriars) friary

The Dominican (Blackfriars) friary was founded some time before 1256 by Sir Roger de Holishe and was built fairly close to the original site of the Greyfriars Friary. There were 24 friars listed there in 1277.

In 1384, when the buildings were threatened by the sea, the monks were granted a licence to move the friary to Blythburgh; however, they remained at Dunwich until the friary was suppressed in November 1538. The property was granted to John Eyre, an auditor of the Court of Augmentation. There are no remains of the friary, because the ruins were engulfed by the sea.

Scandals at Blackfriars

Thomas Hopman, one of the Dominican friars, was in trouble in 1355 for leaving the country without permission. It's thought that he was acting as the Bishop of Ely's agent at the court in Rome in a row between the king and the pope. When he returned, in August, a writ was issued for his arrest, and he was to be sent to the prior at Blackfriars in Dunwich.

Greyfriars Priory

The ruins of Greyfriars Priory (OS grid reference TM 4777 7036) are the remains of the Franciscan friary: the precinct wall, two gatehouses, and the south range of the cloister (which possibly includes the refectory).

It was founded by Richard Fitz-John and his wife Alice at some point before 1277. The original priory was built nearer to the sea, but was destroyed in the storm of 1286 and rebuilt on its present site in 1290.

As with the Dominican Friary, it was dissolved in 1538 and the property was granted to John Eyre.

The site was used as an anti-aircraft battery during the Second World War.

The gatehouse at Dunwich Greyfriars. Photograph by author.

The House of the Knights Templar

King John confirmed the lands and liberties of the preceptory of the Knights Templar in the first year of his reign (1199–1200). When the Templars were suppressed in 1312, the property of the house was given to the Knights

The refectory at Dunwich Greyfriars. Photograph by author.

Remains of Dunwich Greyfriars; plate from Alfred Inigo Suckling's The History and Antiquities of the County of Suffolk, *1846-8. Photograph by author.*

Hospitallers. The building was used until the order of the Hospitallers was suppressed in 1540; the Crown then took the revenues of its manor, and the lands were granted to Thomas Andrews in 1562.

H. Rider Haggard's medieval adventure story *Red Eve*, published in 1911, was set partly at the house of the Knights Templar in Dunwich.

The Ghosts of Dunwich

Unsurprisingly, given that so much of it has been lost to the sea, Dunwich has been called the 'British Atlantis'. One of the most common stories is that at midnight you can hear the church bells ring under the sea (despite the fact that the buildings fell off a cliff and were smashed to pieces rather than being submerged whole).

Naturally, monks have been seen in the ruins; also, 'strange shapes' are said to haunt the area which was formerly a leper colony.

And, given that nearby Blythburgh is so deeply associated with the story of Black Shuck (see page 7), it's not surprising that the dog has been seen in the area; allegedly, a large phantom dog was seen in the ruins of Greyfriars in 1926.

Love stories, too, have their remnants at Dunwich; man apparently walks the cliff paths by the priory, looking for his wife, who eloped with someone else. And another broken-hearted ghost walks the woodland paths: the brother of the lord of the manor, who fell in love with a servant girl who worked at Greyfriars. When he was forbidden to see her again, he died from a broken heart. It's not clear whether the squire who races round the heathland on horseback, on nights when there's a full moon, is the man's brother.

And one of Suffolk scholar M.R. James's best-known ghost stories, *Oh, Whistle and I'll Come to You, My Lad*, was filmed partly on the beach at Dunwich (although the original story was actually set in a fictionalised Felixstowe).

Secret tunnels

As with many monastic buildings, there are legends of a secret tunnel; in the case of Dunwich, it's meant to lead from the priory to the Ship Inn, about 200 yards away, and allegedly allowed the friars to sneak out to the inn. There's allegedly a bricked-up entrance in the cellars of the pub to corroborate the story; but it's also worth remembering that the Ship Inn was once the haunt of smugglers, who would also have appreciated a tunnel...

The Ship Inn, Dunwich. Photograph by author.

Eye Castle

Remains of Eye Castle, showing the windmill that predated the folly; plate from Thomas Kitson Cromwell's Excursions Through Suffolk, *1818-9. Photograph by author.*

Motte and bailey of Eye castle, with fragment of wall from Kerrison's Folly.

Eye Castle (OS grid reference TM 147 738) is an 11th-century motte and bailey, with the remains of a wall from a folly built on the site. Eye Castle is the only castle in Suffolk that's mentioned in the Domesday Book survey of 1086, and was the central feature of the town. It was built on the only high ground in North Suffolk, though obviously the natural mound was augmented to improve the defensive position. Below the motte was the inner bailey, known as Castle Hill; the outer bailey stretched for 120 metres east to west and 70 metres north to south, roughly equivalent to the lines of Church Street, Castle Street and Broad Street. The site is open to the public.

The beginnings of the castle

The Honour of Eye (i.e. a group of about 120 manors) was originally held by Edric of Laxfield, Edward the Confessor's falconer. Edric was the third-largest landholder in Suffolk.

In 1068, William the Conqueror gave the Honour of Eye to William Malet, who had fought with him at Hastings; legend also has it that William was entrusted with the temporary burial of King Harold at Battle after William's victory.

The first castle in Ely was built from wood; William Malet also revised the town layout and set up a market, which effectively took most of the trade from nearby Hoxne (see page 87). When William died fighting Hereward the Wake in 1071, his son Robert, the Sheriff of Suffolk, inherited the castle and continued the building in stone. Robert also founded the Benedictine priory at Eye (see page 60).

William Malet and Hereward the Wake

Hereward the Wake (meaning 'watchful') had been made an outlaw by Edward the Confessor in 1062 for rebellion. He returned home after the Conquest to discover that his father was dead; worse, his brother had been killed and his head nailed above the door, and the Norman lord Peter de Bourne had taken over his family's lands. (There's a strong parallel here with the legend of Robin Hood.) Hereward killed fourteen Normans single-handedly with his sword – the fantastically named 'Brainbiter' – and nailed their heads in place of his brother's; and then he led a band of men in resistance to William the Conqueror.

The Danish king Swein Estrithson sent an army to establish a camp on the Isle of Ely; Hereward and his men joined them. In 1070, Hereward attacked and looted Peterborough Abbey, claiming that he wanted to save the treasures from the Normans. William didn't take the resistance lightly and sent his men to besiege the island; Malet, as the Sheriff of Suffolk, took part in the siege, and was killed during a skirmish.

William ordered his men to build a causeway across the marshes to the island, though all three of their attempts failed. On one occasion, the mile-long causeway sank under the weight of the horses and armour. Another time, Hereward had left the island by a secret path and infiltrated William's camp at Brandon, disguised as a potter; he overheard the plans for invasion, so he knew exactly what William was going to do and how to counteract it. When William's men built the causeway, Hereward's men hid among the reeds and set fire to the vegetation. The Normans were burned alive; those who managed to escape the flames drowned, or were shot by Hereward's archers.

William then decided to take a sneakier route – or maybe the monks at Ely had just had enough of the siege and were easy to sway. One of his knights managed to bribe a monk who lived on the island to show them a safe route across the marshes. The Normans captured Ely, and it's believed that Hereward escaped and was able to continue his resistance.

One 12th-century chronicle, *Gesta Herewardi*, says that William eventually pardoned Hereward; the Norman chronicler Geoffrey Gaimar adds that, after the pardon, Hereward moved to France and was eventually murdered by the Normans.

Riots and rebellions

Robert Malet, who inherited his father's estates as well as his office of the Sheriff of Suffolk, was one of the largest landowners in Norman England. According to the Domesday book he held 221 manors in Suffolk, 32 in Yorkshire and 14 in four other counties, as well as family property in Normandy.

In 1075, Robert was involved in suppressing the rebellion of Ralph de Guader at Norwich Castle.

When William the Conqueror died in 1087, his kingdom was split between his two eldest sons: Robert Curthose, the Duke of Normandy, and William Rufus. Robert Curthose planned to invade England and take the throne; Robert Malet had clearly fallen out with William Rufus, as he supported the Duke of Normandy. William Rufus retaliated by taking the lordship of Eye from Malet at some time before 1094, and Malet left the country. However, on William Rufus's death, Malet returned to England and was one of the witnesses on Henry I's coronation charter. The lordship of Eye was restored to him by Henry I, and Malet became the Great Chamberlain of England .

Some sources suggest that Malet then fell out with Henry and was executed in 1106; others say that he was killed in the battle of Tinchebray, where Henry I's forces captured Robert Curthose and imprisoned him.

Robert's successor was William Malet – the relationship isn't entirely clear, but he was thought to be Robert's son, nephew or possibly his younger brother. William Malet was banished around 1110 for plotting against the king, and the castle was transferred to Stephen (Henry I's heir).

The castle was attacked by Hugh Bigod in October 1173 as part of his rebellion against Henry II, just after he'd destroyed the castle at Haughley (see page 78). Bigod failed to capture Eye, but his forces did much damage to the fabric of the castle and it was rebuilt and strengthened in 1186.

In 1265, the castle was attacked again, during the rebellion of the Barons.

The End of the Castle

In 1272, the castle reverted to the Crown, and in 1331 it was given to Edward III's brother. By 1370 it was in ruins; much of the stone was reused elsewhere in the town, but the remaining building was used as a prison.

In 1561, a windmill was built on the site. The Kerrison family bought the land in 1823 and demolished the windmill in 1844. They built a Victorian imitation of the old castle keep, which was known locally as Kerrison's Folly; it contained a house for General Sir Edward Kerrison's batsman, who saved his life at Waterloo in 1815. The folly was used as local museum until 1917. It was badly damaged by a storm in the 1960s, and the building gradually decayed into its present-day ruinous state.

Roman Finds

In 1781, some labourers were digging in a field near the castle and discovered a box made of lead. The box contained several hundred gold Roman coins, mainly showing the late 4th-century emperors Arcadius and Honorius.

Eye Priory

E ye Priory (OS grid reference TM 1524 7406) was a Benedictine priory founded by Robert Malet (see Eye Castle, page 57) in around 1080 and dedicated to St Peter. The only remains are the gatehouse, used as a barn, which is on private land and is not open to the public.

Beginnings of the Priory

The priory was originally an 'alien' priory and was a subordinate priory of Bernay in Normandy, meaning that the prior and the monks could only be at Eye by permission of the prior of Bernay. Although its foundation was very lavish, by 1385, it could only support three or four monks and the priory asked for denization (i.e. they would be considered English and would no longer have to pay subsidies to the crown).

Arguments with Bernay

Hervey of Leon – who at the time was the patron of the priory – wrote to King Stephen and the Bishop of Norwich in 1396. He said that the monks at Eye had been disturbed by the interference of Bernay, particularly by having monks and the prior moved about. He suggested that the way forward would be to agree that, provided Eye remained a priory and not an abbey, the Lord of Eye could appoint the prior, and the only way the abbot of Bernay could remove him would be if the prior had committed a crime. The abbot also couldn't move the monks about without the agreement of the prior, and could stay at Eye only for a month, with a maximum of seven horses for himself, his monks and his servants; and the priory was to pay him 10,000 herrings at Dunwich before Advent.

The Red Book of Eye

At one point the priory had a cell or subordinate small priory at Dunwich (see page 52); however, the building was swept away by the sea. One of the possessions they managed to rescue was St Felix's book of the gospels, known as the 'Red Book of Eye'.

People used to swear oaths on the book. At Dissolution, the commissioners recorded it as 'an old masse boke called the redde boke of Eye garnysshed with a lytell sylver on the one side, the residewe lytell worth, xxd'. The twenty pence referred to the worth of a silver corner of the book; although the commissioners regarded the book itself as worthless, it was actually priceless! The 16th-century antiquary John Leland saw the book and reported that it was written in Lombardic characters; there were also records of the book in the Corporation of Eye in the 18th century. Sadly, the book is now lost; the antiquary M.R. James wrote in 1930 that he'd heard that the book had been cut up for 'game labels' at Brome Hall, though he added that his enquiries had revealed nothing.

Scandals

At most of the bishop's visitations, the monks said that 'omnia bene' – all was well. However, in 1514, when Bishop Nix visited, he made an injunction that Margery the washerwoman wasn't allowed to go into the priory, and the prior had to get some books back that he'd lent to Dr White before Christmas and make proper accounts.

However, there was still clearly a problem, because at the visitation of 1520 all eight monks said that they had suspicions about the prior, Richard Bettys, and his dealings with Margery Verre (it's tempting to speculate that she was the former washerwoman).They also said that he'd sold silver bowls belonging to the priory, and hadn't produced any accounts since he became prior.

At the next visitation, in 1526, all was well apart from the fact that the common seal (used on legal documents) was kept in a chest with only one key; usually, a chest was locked with three keys kept by three different people, so the contents couldn't be removed and misused.

End of the Priory

The priory was dissolved in 1537 and the site was granted to the Duke of Suffolk. William Parker, the prior, was given a pension of £18.

Felixstowe Landguard Fort

Felixstowe Landguard Fort (OS map reference TM 28373 31915) is the remainder of an 18th century fort; it marks the spot where England was last invaded, in 1667. It is in the care of the Landguard Fort Trust (on behalf of English Heritage) and is open to the public.

Felixstowe Landguard Fort: the original 18th-century walls with a cream brick facade on the gateway. Photograph by author.

The Beginning of the Fort

The fort was built between 1540 and 1545 as two earth bulwarks (which, together with the three at Harwich, cost the king's engineers £2,717) and two blockhouses; they decayed very quickly, so the guns went back to the Tower of London in 1552. The fort was rebuilt in 1624-8 as a square structure of earth, reinforced by wood and with a bastion in each corner. It was repaired in 1666, and a brick wall was built around it.

The government was short of money in the 17th century – which meant that in turn the soldiers were short of food and supplies. Colonel Henry Farre complained in 1661 that his men only had bread and cheese to eat, and although he commanded

112 men they had only 20 beds between them, so most of the men were forced to sleep on the floor.

The mutiny of 1628

There was a mutiny among the soldiers in 1628 – mainly due to arrears of pay. It was quickly stopped, and the commander of the fort, Captain Gosnold, let the men draw lots so that only one man would be punished. Benjamin Dammont was sent to prison at Woodbridge, but when he reached Trimley the constable there took pity on him and let him go.

The Invasion of the Dutch

In June 1667, the Dutch had already attacked the English fleet in the Medway and destroyed the fort at Sheerness. On 2 July 1667, they attacked Harwich and 12 of Admiral de Ruyter's warships tried to bomb Landguard Fort – but they couldn't get close enough. Then de Ruyter ordered a force of around 800 men to land on Felixstowe beach; the force included musketeers, pikemen, sailors (grenadiers) and small cannon. They were led by Colonel Thomas Dolman, an English professional soldier who had once served with Cromwell but changed sides.

Twice, the Dutch force tried to attack the fort; however, Captain Nathanial Darrell, with a garrison of only 200 (including musketeers from the Duke of York and Albany's Maritime Regiment of Foot – the forerunner of the English Marines), beat them back. Darrell's men's musket-fire meant that the Dutch couldn't cross the fort ditch, and a small English warship sent cannon fire to the beach, scattering the shingle. In the end, the Dutch retreated, leaving eight dead – whereas in the fort there was only one fatality and Darrell had a shoulder-wound.

The Building of the Present-day Fort

The 17th-century fort was pulled down in 1716 and a new battery and fort were built; then in 1745 a new pentagonal-shaped fort with bastions was built just to the north of the old site. New batteries were constructed in the 1750s and in 1780; then in 1871-5 it was extensively remodelled, with the interior barracks rebuilt as a keep and in 1878

Felixstowe Landguard Fort. Photograph by author.

a new block with an observation room and main building (called the Ravelin) was built for submarine mining. New batteries were built in 1901 to house modern guns when the fort's arms became outdated.

Felixstowe Landguard Fort, interior. Photograph by author.

The Fort in the First World War

During the war, ships coming in and out of the haven at Harwich were controlled by a Port War Signal Station which was part of the Fire Commander's Post on the roof of Landguard Fort. There were air attacks in July 1917 which saw 7 dead, 22 wounded and much damage at the Royal Naval Air Station in Felixstowe; but perhaps the most unusual event the harbour at Felixstowe and Harwich saw during the war was when 122 German U-boats surrendered to Admiral Tyrwhitt in November 1918. The terms and conditions were:

- The boat was to be in an efficient condition, with periscopes, main motors, diesel engines, and auxiliary engines in good working order.
- The boat was to be in surface trim, with all diving tanks blown.
- The torpedoes were to be on board, without their war-heads, and the torpedoes were to be clear of the tubes.
- The wireless was to be complete.
- There were to be no explosives on board.
- There were to be no booby traps or infernal machines on board.

The ships in the harbour were crowded with spectators when the first batch arrived on 20 November 1918, but everyone was silent as the German submarines – with the British crew to whom they'd surrendered – hoisted the white flag of surrender and slowly sailed out of the mist and into the harbour.

The Fort in the Second World War and after

The fort was one of the balloon launch sites of Operation Outward. In the operation, thousands of hydrogen balloons were sent to Germany, carrying either bombs or trailing steel wires that would damage power lines.

During the Cold War, in 1951, two of the gun casemates were made into a control room. However, five years later, the Coastal Artillery was disbanded and the fort was no longer needed. It was abandoned and sealed up; eventually, it came into the care of English Heritage, which made the structures safe in 1997-8 and opened the fort to the public.

Scandals: Captain Philip Thicknesse

Captain Philip Thicknesse was the Lieutenant-Governor of Landguard Fort between 1753 and 1766. Although the *Gentlemen's Magazine* in 1809 said of him, 'In point of person he was extremely handsome; his conversation was entertaining, his talents undisputed, his manners elegant and fascinating; he excelled in all the accomplishments of the day', Thicknesse was a very volatile character and the men at the fort found him to be an arrogant bully with a foul temper. (And in fact the *Gentlemen's Magazine* also admitted that Thicknesse 'was susceptible in the extreme of everything that bordered on insult and rudeness' – unsurprisingly, his memoirs in 1790 became a bestseller.)

In 1761, Thicknesse pressed charges against Captain William Lynch, saying that he'd gone absent without leave during wartime – even though Lynch wasn't under Thicknesse's command. A Court Martial was held at the fort in September 1761, and found Lynch not guilty. Thicknesse lost his temper in court, and was reprimanded for his loss of temper. But it didn't cool him: he began lambasting Colonel Francis Vernon, the president of the trial, and then published scandalous broadsheets to try to scupper Vernon's hopes of being elected to Parliament. Vernon took him to court; at the assizes in Bury St Edmunds in August 1763 he was found guilty of slander. He was given a three-month jail sentence and a £100 fine, and had to find sureties for seven years' good behaviour.

But his sentence clearly didn't subdue him; on his return to the fort, he pressed charges against another officer who'd been in command during his absence. The situation deteriorated rapidly, and Thicknesse found himself on trial again in July 1765; he was found guilty and sentenced to a public reprimand.

September saw him back at the fort, but the War Office said he was unfit to command and shouldn't live there. Thicknesse finally took the hint and resigned in 1766. He went back to Bath – where he'd formerly gambled a lot and indulged in laudanum – and wrote a guide to the area, where he recommended drinking to excess and 'the frequent inhalation of the breath of young women' (!). He continued picking quarrels with people, including painter Thomas Gainsborough, and disowned his two sons.

He died near Boulogne on 23 November 1792 and was buried there. His will contained a very unusual and rather grim bequest: he wanted his right hand cut off and delivered to his son, Lord Audley, 'in hopes that such a sight may remind him of his duty to God after having so long abandoned the duty he owed to a father, who once affectionately loved him'.

The Ghosts of Felixstowe Landguard Fort

A ghostly coach pulled by a team of horses is said to cross a ditch next to the fort, where there used to be a drawbridge. There were also reports during the 1990s of visitors seeing a sailor looking out of one of the windows, lights in the fort at night, and peopled feeling as if they were pushed when visiting the upper floors of the fort.

One ghost that haunts the fort is a lone musketeer; soldiers during Second World War saw him marching along a rampart, and dogs are said to avoid the area. It's thought that he was the only Englishman who lost his life during the Dutch invasion, and it's also thought that he only appears when the country is in danger.

There's also the ghost of a lady, Maria, who cries in grief and whispers in Portuguese. So the story goes, in the middle of the 18th century, the paymaster sergeant married a Portuguese woman, Maria. The other wives at the fort didn't like her; one day in 1757, when a silk handkerchief went missing, they blamed Maria. The paymaster sergeant was convinced of her innocence and when he was told to deal with the situation, he left the fort to find help to prove that Maria didn't steal the handkerchief. When he came back, four days later, he was accused of desertion and the fort's firing squad executed him in the dry moat. Maria was driven mad by grief and threw herself off the ramparts, killing herself.

Another ghost story dating from the 18th century involves a young man who'd been on duty overseas; while abroad, he caught a tropical disease. The symptoms only came out after he arrived back at the fort, and his body was covered with pustules. The medical officer, fearing that the men in the fort would panic about the plague being among them, agreed with four other officers to keep the lad's condition a secret from the rest of the fort, and confined the sick man to a locked, darkened room. The soldier died, and it's said that he can still be heard, crying for his mother.

During visits by mediums, a ghost was discovered in the bathroom: a young soldier who died during the First World War. There's no documentary evidence to support the claim, but the soldier either hit his head on the bath when a practical joke went wrong, or was killed when he was caught stealing from friends. It's said that one of the soldiers involved in the death felt so guilty about his part in the death and the cover-up that he hanged himself in the magazine room – and his ghost still haunts the area.

Felixstowe - Walton Castle

The remains of Walton Castle in Felixstowe (OS grid reference TM 434357) lie off the coast of Felixstowe, after being undermined by the sea in the 18th century. At very low tide, part of the wall was still visible in the early part of this century.

From Roman fortress ...

Walton Castle is one of the two forts tentatively identified with the Roman fort of Othona, listed in the *Notitia Dignitatum* (the other candidate is Bradwell, in Essex). The Saxon shore fort system – named after the Count of the Saxon Shore, a senior commander in the Roman Army – stretched between Brancaster in Norfolk to Portchester in Hampshire, and protected the coastline against pirates, raids or invasions. The walls enclosed an area of around six acres, and the castle was built between 276 and 285; it was originally sited about 30 metres above sea level. The legions were recalled to Italy in 410, and after that the Saxons took over the fort.

... to ancient Christian see ...

Like Dunwich, Felixstowe has been associated with the name of Dommoc (sometimes known as Dunmoc); Bede, the early 8th-century historian, said that Dommoc was the site of the first East Anglian episcopal minster and was given to St Felix by Sigeberht, who ruled from 630 to 635.

... to Norman Castle

The Roman fort was reused by the Normans. After 1066, the land was given to Roger Bigod; he used the fort as the bailey for his castle. The castle was then strengthened by his son, Hugh.

As with the other Bigod castles, Walton was part of a power struggle during the reigns of Stephen and Henry II. In 1140, Stephen attacked Walton Castle before defeating Hugh Bigod at Bungay, and in 1157 Henry II confiscated the castle and garrisoned it.

On 29 September 1173 Earl of Leicester sailed to Walton with an army of Flemish mercenaries; they'd been resisted at Dunwich (see page 51), but Hugh Bigod gave him hospitality at Framlingham. They besieged several castles in the area; but the castle at Walton withstood the siege. Bigod, Leicester and their army then went to Fornham (see Ipswich Castle on page 92 for the full story), where they were thoroughly routed.

In 1176, Henry II dismantled Walton Castle and it's said that he used the stone to build his castle at Orford (see page 123); however, Thomas Kitson Cromwell, writing in 1819, said the stone was used to make footpaths on both sides of the roads in Felixstowe, Walton and Trimley. The Pipe Rolls of 1176 say that some of the stone was sold in Ipswich. However, the walls of the Roman fort clearly survived the demolition, because they were recorded as still standing before they fell into the sea in the early 18th century. Cromwell says that the minutes of the Antiquarian Society in 1722 describes a wall on the cliff between the Landguard Fort and Woodbridge river, which was 100 yards long, 5 feet high and 12 feet thick, made from pebbles and Roman bricks; there were also several pieces of wall on the beach which had clearly fallen over the cliff, and 'at low-water mark very much of the like is visible at some distance in the sea'. He adds that another description, from 1740, said that the remains of the wall on the west side was 187 yards long and 9 feet thick. R. G. Collingwood, writing in 1930, described a drawing from 1623 which showed cylindrical bastions at the corners of the castle.

Investigations

Underwater teams investigated the area in 1933, 1970 and 1976. Finds included coins dating from AD14 to the 4th century.

Felixstowe Priory

St Mary's church, Walton, Felixstowe. Photograph by author.

Felixstowe Priory (OS grid reference TM 295 356) was a Benedictine priory which was founded by Roger Bigod in about 1097. In 1105, he gave the priory to St Andrew's monastery in Rochester as a cell or dependent priory (which is where the confusion about the date of the priory has come in; some sources say that the priory was founded in 1105).

The original endowment of the monastery included 100 acres within the Roman enclosure at Walton (see page 67), and the monastery was described as being built at 'Fylthestow' (which was the Saxon for 'a place where hay grows' or 'place of felled trees'). As the priory was dedicated to St Felix, the name of the town and changed over the years to Felixstow, and the final E of Felixstowe was added in the 19th century when the town became a fashionable seaside resort.

Floods

In 1146 the monastery gave their lands within the Roman enclosure back to the Bigods; in exchange he gave them land near Walton church. In 1178, the monks built and additional refectory, dormitory and guest house on to the priory; there were about a dozen monks living at the priory.

But, as with many towns on the east coast, the area was subject to erosion by the North Sea. By the 1290s, the buildings within the priory compound were flooded at every high tide. The monks had had enough of fighting against the inevitable, and moved the priory to their land near Walton Church. Nowadays, the site of the original priory is about a mile out to sea.

Scandals

In the late 1290s, it was discovered that the prior of Walton had been altering leases of properties given to the priory without the permission of the prior at Rochester. So when the monks moved to the new

Fragmentary medieval remains at St Mary's church, Walton, Felixstowe. Photograph by author.

buildings, the prior at Rochester said that the new building would be for four monks only, and they would have a warden rather than a prior – effectively, they were demoted.

The Rising of 1381

The Rising of 1381 (often known as the Peasants' Revolt) had very complex causes – and the revolt included leaders of manorial communities as well as peasants, so it wasn't just the 'peasants' revolt'. At the time the country was recovering from the impact of the Black Death, which had a death rate of around a third to half the population and led to incredible hardships among the poor. The church still insisted on collecting tithes, despite the fact that parishioners were starving. Just as villeins were starting to negotiate their freedom and the freemen were negotiating higher wages (some by moving to wherever the highest rates would be paid), the king passed the Statute of Labourers which decreed that there would be no wage rises for the freemen and no freedom for the villeins, and nobody was allowed to move away from their villages.

There were unpopular poll taxes from 1377 to 1381 to help pay for the war against France; the last one was a shilling per head, nearly a week's wages for the peasant, and the tax was the same for everyone regardless of income. Many people hid rather than paying taxes, but the king announced he would be sending out new tax collectors and those who had evaded the tax would be punished. The people started to rebel. Tax collectors were attacked, and property of the church and the nobility was destroyed. Led by Wat Tyler, the rebels burned tax records and marched to London to demand fair treatment from the king – in particular, fair wages, the end of market monopolies and an end to the feudal system.

In Suffolk, the priory Felixstowe was badly damaged in the revolt; locally, the revolt was led by John Battisford, who was the parson at nearby Bucklesham. He attacked Walton Manor and burned the court rolls, and also burned the court rolls of Felixstowe Priory, along with the warden's house. The earliest court rolls that survive date from 1382, and refer to the expenses of repairing the manor house.

Suppression

In 1528, the priory was suppressed; it was intended that the revenues would be used towards building Wolsey's college in Ipswich (see page 101), but after Wolsey's fall from grace building stopped and the college was shut. In 1532, the lands were granted to Thomas Howard, the 3rd Duke of Norfolk, and later given to Thomas Seckford by Elizabeth I.

Ruins and excavations

The manor house and the priory both fell into ruin; a 17th century manuscript says that the author saw the stone ruins of Felixstowe Hall and the priory. Priory House was demolished in 1810.

The site was excavated in 1968. A quantity of stained glass was found, as well as flint flakes and some few sherds of Roman/British pottery and roof tiles. Some of the tile and stone was probably used in the structure of St Mary's church and a fragment of medieval ruins is still visible in the churchyard. A further excavation in 1971 resulted in the discovery of the foundations of the old manor house.

Flixton Priory

Flixton Priory (OS grid reference TM 3153 8638) is the remains of an Augustinian nunnery, in the grounds of Abbey Farm. The farmhouse is thought to incorporate some of the remains of the church. The priory itself was cloistered and also had a moat; part of the wall of the south range can still be seen, along with earthworks. The remains are on private land and are not accessible to the public.

The beginnings of the priory

The Augustinian nunnery was founded by the widow Margery de Creke in 1258, dedicated to the Blessed Virgin and St Catherine and originally intended for eighteen nuns. After the Black Death, its income and the number of nuns halved and it never really recovered.

The records of the priory showed that much of their income went in caring for the poor. They also looked after their former prioress, Katharine Pilly, who resigned in 1432 after 18 years as prioress because she was old and blind. In 1433, the bishop's visitation said that she should have a room for herself and her maid, and each week they should be given two white loaves, eight loaves of 'hool' bread (whole bread), and eight gallons of convent beer, as well as the same meal that the nuns had in the refectory. She was also given 200 faggots, 100 logs and eight pounds of candles a year, and it was directed that one of the nuns, Cecelia Creyke, should sit with her at mealtimes and also read divine service to her daily.

Scandals

The visitations all seemed to go well until August 1514, when Bishop Nix visited. Several nuns complained that the prioress, Margaret Punder, was capricious and severe; they also said that she let discipline and administration slide, and saw rather too much of John Wells (the chaplain, who was a relative). The bishop ordered that John Wells should leave the town by All Saints' Day (1 November).

In August 1520, Alice Wright, the prioress, said that Margaret Punder was disobedient – and Margeret in turn said that she wasn't getting her proper pension, board or winter fuel. The sub-prioress said that the prioress didn't give annual accounts, and four of the nuns said that when they were ill, the prioress still made them get up for the service of Mattins. The prioress explained that she wasn't used to figures and hadn't written down what she'd spent; Nicholas Carr, the chancellor of the diocese, told her that if she didn't give yearly accounts she'd be thrown out. Clearly there were other problems, because his other injunctions were that all the dogs bar one had to be removed from the priory within a month, and the prioress had to have another nun with her if she slept outside the dormitory. In addition, she had to dismiss Richard Carr.

Flixton Hall; plate from Alfred Inigo Suckling's The History and Antiquities of the County of Suffolk, *1846-8. Photograph by author.*

From then on, the visitations ran smoothly again.

Suppression

The nunnery was listed for suppression in 1528 but wasn't actually dissolved until 1536. In 1537 the lands were granted to Richard Warton. Some of the materials from the priory (including the windows and porch from the church) were used by Mr Tasburgh to build an extension to his house, St Peter's Hall in South Elmham, near Bungay (now St Peter's Brewery); the work was completed in summer 1539 and he held a feast in the great hall to celebrate.

The Tasburgh family ended up owning the site of the priory and built Flixton Hall within the ruins. When Charles II visited the hall, he allegedly said, 'these popish dogs [the Tasburghs were Catholics] have a beautiful kennel'. The house was gutted in a fire in 1846, and although it was restored it was finally demolished in 1950.

Framlingham Castle

Framlingham castle. Photograph by author.

Framlingham Castle (OS grid reference TN 287637) is the remains of the 12th-century castle owned by the Bigods, built on the site of an earlier castle; there is a stone curtain wall and 13 mural towers. It is in the care of English Heritage and is open to the public.

The beginnings of the castle

There was a settlement at Framlingham during Saxon times, though little is known apart about it from the fact that there were three manors, and a Saxon cemetery containing 48 skeletons was excavated in 1954 next to the footpath leading to the castle gate. Some

Framlingham castle ditches. Photograph by author.

Remains of Framlingham Castle; plate from Thomas Kitson Cromwell's Excursions
Through Suffolk, *1818-9. Photograph by author.*

historians believe that the original castle was built by Raedwald in the early
seventh century, but there is no evidence of the building.

The first record of Framlingham Castle is in 1101 when Henry I granted the
manor to Roger Bigod – although Roger may have had the site as early as 1086.
Roger built a motte and bailey castle, of which only the bailey survives today. He
put a wooden tower on the motte, roughly in the place where the poorhouse stands
now.

Roger's son Hugh was made the Earl of Norfolk and Suffolk in 1140 by King
Stephen. However, Hugh fell out with Stephen (see page 13) and eventually helped
Matilda's son Henry II accede the throne. When Henry gave him a charter
confirming his plans in 1155, Hugh rebuilt the hall and the chapel in stone.

Sieges – and fights with the the king

As Hugh's power base grew, he continued to fight with the king. In 1156 he took
part in an uprising – and when Henry II crushed the rebellion, he confiscated
Hugh's lands and castle and a Royal garrison was stationed at Framlingham.

In 1164, Henry gave the castle back to the Bigods. He also started building
Orford Castle (see page 123) in an attempt to limit Hugh's power base.
Unsurprisingly, Hugh ended up in strife with the king again, in 1173, when he
backed Prince Henry's rebellion against his father. They failed to capture Walton or
Orford, but marched from Framlingham to Haughley (see page 83).

When the rebellion was put down, Henry had had enough. Again, he confiscated the Bigod lands, but this time he paid Alnodus, the royal engineer, to demolish Framlingham Castle. Hugh died in 1177, still out of favour with the king.

Henry refused to make Hugh's son Roger the Earl of Norfolk; but when Richard I came to the throne in 1189 he gave Roger the title and his lands back. Roger rebuilt the castle at Framlingham, adding the curtain walls with 12 towers, each having walls almost 8 feet thick. Each tower could be sealed off and defended; and the top of each tower had a fighting gallery, which was reached by a ladder from the wall walk. Roger entertained King John there in 1213 – but he was also one of the Barons who forced John to sign the Magna Carta (see page 27). However, when the Magna Carta failed, the country was plunged into civil war. In March 1216, John besieged the castle with foreign mercenaries. Roger's garrison had only 53 fighting men – 26 knights, 20 sergeants, and seven crossbow men – as well as a chaplain and three servants, and they surrendered after two days.

The castle was returned to the Bigods the following year, when Henry III came to the throne, and the family held the castle for the rest of the century.

However, Roger, the fifth Earl of Norfolk, fell out badly with Edward I in 1297. The king told him he had to lead an army to fight the French in Gascony, and Roger replied that he wasn't bound to go unless the king was would be there too, leading him. Edward was furious, and roared, 'By God, Sir Earl, you shall go or hang.' Roger kept his cool: 'By God, O King, I will neither go nor hang.' Roger didn't go to Gascony, and he wasn't hanged – but the King confiscated his lands and sacked him as Marshal. Roger died in 1306, in debt, the last of the Bigods. His estates passed to the Crown, and Framlingham Castle eventually went to Thomas Mowbray, who was made the Duke of Norfolk in 1397 after he confessed his involvement in a plot to seize Richard II and helped to bring the rest of the conspirators to justice. However, Thomas was then exiled for rebelling against Henry V.

Mary Tudor, Elizabeth I and the Howards

The castle passed to the Howard family in 1480. Sir John Howard was a close ally of Richard III, who made him the Duke of Norfolk in 1483. The castle was refurbished about this time, but in 1485 John Howard was killed at the Battle of Bosworth. His son Thomas was thrown into the tower of London by Henry VII and the castle given to John de Vere, but it was returned to Thomas in 1489. The first Duke of Norfolk, another Thomas Howard, was involved in arranging the marriage between Henry and his niece Anne Boleyn, and took her part when she fell from grace. The Duke himself fell from favour when Henry's marriage to another of his nieces, Catherine Howard, failed.

Thomas's son Henry was executed for treason in 1546; he was the last person hanged by Henry VIII. Thomas was also implicated in the treason, so he was thrown in prison and his lands were seized. He was saved from the scaffold when Henry VIII died the day before Thomas was due to be executed; he was left in prison and the castle passed to Edward VI. Edward gave it to his sister Mary Tudor in 1553.

Mary stayed at Framlingham, with her flag flying from the castle while she waited to hear who would succeed to the crown after Edward died. Thirteen thousand supporters camped round the castle, and finally the Earl of Arundel came to confirm that she was the queen. On 20 July 1553 she gave her first royal command from Framlingham.

Thomas Howard was finally released from prison and Framlingham Castle was returned to his family; he died the following year, and his grandson (also Thomas) was executed for treason in 1572 because he had planned to marry Mary Queen of Scots and overthrow Elizabeth. His son Philip had been thrown in the Tower of London for being a Catholic, and died there in 1595. Framlingham had already started to decay, and the queen planned to use it as a prison for Catholic priests; however, because the castle had decayed so much, the priests temporarily had to find lodgings in the village!

The end of the castle

In 1635 the castle was sold to Sir Robert Hitcham for £14,000 (the equivalent of one and three-quarter million pounds in modern terms); he left it in his will to the master and fellows of Pembroke College, Cambridge, on condition that the castle was pulled down and a poor house was built. It took a while to sort out his will, but in 1664 the workhouse was built. In 1665, it was used to house the victims of the plague, and then it fell out of use for a few years. It was reopened in 1699 for children; the children were set to work spinning wool, but were also taught reading, writing and arithmetic for two hours a day. The parish poorhouse was used until 1835, when a new poorhouse was built at Wickham Market.

After the poor house was closed, the castle had several uses – as a store, the county courthouse, the parish meeting hall, a fire station, a drill hall and assembly rooms. In 1913, Pembroke College gave the castle to the state and it became a national monument. It has been cared for by English Heritage since 1984.

Framlingham castle interior.
Photograph by author.

ℋaughley Castle

Haughley Castle (OS grid reference TM 025 624) is the remains of an 11th-century castle. It is on private land and not open to the public; however, the wet ditch can be seen around the edge of the churchyard and part of the moat is also visible in the village centre. The motte can be seen from the field behind the church.

Village pond – remainder of the moat at Haughley. Photograph by author.

The beginnings of the castle

Haughley was originally called Hageneth or Hagenorth, and the mound is one of the largest surviving mottes in Britain and is definitely the largest in Suffolk: 26 metres high, 64 metres diameter at the base and 26 metres diameter at the top. The earthworks cover around 7 acres.

It was originally a Druid site, which was taken over as a Roman camp (Sitomagus) following Boudica's rebellion in AD 61. During the Roman period 3,000 men were garrisoned there; they were part of the garrison at Colchester and were led by Suetonius.

Remainder of the mound at Haughley, behind the church – the castle was sited roughly where the cedar tree is. Photograph by author.

The site was reused by the Danes and the Saxons, and the motte was first raised in around 1050. Like Clare, before the Conquest, Haughley was part of the lands of Guthmund; the lands were stripped from him by William the Conqueror and granted to Hugh de Montfort (aka Hugh the Bearded) as one of the three 'Honours' in Suffolk (the others being Clare and Eye – see pages 43 and 57 respectively). An 'honour' was basically a group of manors or estates, and the lord of the manor had the right to crenellate his buildings (i.e. make castles).

William insisted that a castle should be constructed at Haughley; Hugh had to build extra layers onto the motte and make the ditches larger before he could build a wooden castle on the site. Hugh became a monk in 1088 and was succeeded by his son Hugh (II).

However, when William the Conqueror died, he left Normandy to his eldest son, Robert Curthose, and England to his second son, William Rufus. Robert Curthose thought that, as the eldest, he should have had England as well, and prepared to invade England – and the de Montforts, like the Malets of Eye (see page 57), chose to support the wrong side. When Curthose was defeated and imprisoned, Hugh lost Haughley to the Crown, and left with his brother for the Crusades.

The manor passed to Adelize, Hugh's daughter; her second husband, Robert de Vere, was made constable of the castle at some point before 1107, and by then the castle had been rebuilt in flint and stone.

Scandals – trial by combat

Hugh's grandson – also named Hugh – was also involved in a row over the crown. He supported William, the son of Robert Curthose, against Henry I in 1124. Again the de Montforts had chosen the losing side; Hugh was taken prisoner and kept in jail for 14 years.

In the meantime, the manor and the post of constable had passed to Gilbert of Ghent. And when Henry II came to the throne in 1154 the manor went to Robert FitxSusshe, but the post of constable was given to Henry of Essex.

Essex was Henry II's standard bearer at the Battle of Counsylth (Coleshill) in 1157. Apparently, he heard several people cry, 'The King is slain!' – and in response he threw down the standard and fled the field in terror.

Henry II saw Essex's action as the result of fear rather than intentional desertion, and Essex continued as the royal constable; he also served in Toulouse in 1159. But Robert saw his chance to get Haughley Castle back and charged Essex with being a coward and a traitor; he made the point that Roger, the Earl of Clare, had rallied the troops and picked up the standard when Essex had failed. On 31 March 1163, Henry II presided over the Curia Regis at Windsor and Robert formerly appealed (accused) Essex of cowardice. As this was three years before Henry II reformed the law to allow trial by jury at the Assize of Clarendon, this meant that Essex would face trial by ordeal.

In Anglo Saxon England, trial by ordeal took one of four forms. The first was that the accused had to eat a cake of barley bread while a priest prayed; if he was guilty, his face would seize up and he wouldn't be able to chew or swallow. (This sounds innocuous – but the stress of the situation would cause a dry mouth, and trying to eat something dry without any saliva to help you swallow it would indeed make you choke.)

The second was trial by immersion: with a cord round his waist, the accused would be lowered into a pool. If he sank, he was innocent; if he floated, he was guilty.

The third was trial by hot iron: water would be heated in a cauldron in the church, and a piece of iron or a stone would be dropped in the bottom. When the water was at boiling point, the accused had to put his arm into the cauldron and take out the iron or stone. His arm would then be wrapped in a clean cloth and sealed by the church. After three days, the seal would be broken, the bandage unwrapped and his skin inspected. If it was healed, he was innocent.

The fourth was trial by fire, which worked in a very similar way to trial by hot iron. An iron was placed on the fire during mass; at the end of mass, the accused had to take it in his bare hand and carry it for a distance equivalent to nine times the length of his foot.

Then his arm would be wrapped as per the trial by hot iron, and his skin inspected in the same way.

After the Norman Conquest, a fifth ordeal was added: this was trial by combat. Whoever won the battle also won the case. By the mid 12th century, this was the most fashionable form of ordeal – and, in court, the case of de Montfort versus Essex would be settled by trial by combat.

They exchanged gloves as a symbol of faith that both would turn up, and also 'wads' (pledges from neighbours as surety that they would turn up). The king announced that battle would take place on 8 April at Reading; the battleground was at Fry's Island near the Abbey.

In trial by combat, the duelling ground was sixty feet square and the two combatants had a quarterstaff and a shield; combat had to start before noon and end before sunset, and both parties had to swear an oath that they weren't using witchcraft or sorcery. The battle only ended when one of the combatants was dead or disabled – or if they shouted 'craven', but that meant being outlawed.

Sources differ as to what happened next; some say that Essex lay on the ground and pretended to be dead before de Montfort could land his first blow, while others say that the fight took place and de Montfort beat him so badly that the king thought Essex was dead, and told the monks of Reading Abbey to bury him as a traitor.

However, when the monks carried him away, they discovered that he was still alive, and they nursed him back to health. As a traitor, Essex had forfeited his lands, and as a coward he should have forfeited his life; however, the king pardoned Essex on condition that he became a monk. He did so, and told his story to two monks from Bury St Edmund: Abbot Sampson and Jocelin de Brakelond.

Essex claimed that during the battle he'd seen a vision that paralysed him: St Edmund and the knight Gilbert de Cereville had both appeared next to Robert de Montfort. He said then that it was divine retribution: he'd cheated the abbey at Bury St Edmunds, because he'd tried a criminal in his court at Haughley for an offence committed within the abbey of St Edmund's grounds, and hadn't paid the abbey a fine. As for Gilbert: Essex's wife claimed that the knight had made advances to her, so Essex threw him in prison, put him in chains and slowly tortured him until he died. Except Gilbert was innocent: Essex's wife had made the advances and, when Gilbert spurned them, decided to get her revenge.

Although de Montfort had expected Henry II to return Haughley to him after his victory against Essex, he was disappointed – the king kept the lands.

Randolph de Broc and the murder of Thomas Becket

Randolph de Broc became constable of Haughley; he also held Saltwood Castle in Kent, which had belonged to Thomas Becket, the Archbishop of Canterbury and the former Lord Chancellor. Henry II and Becket came to blows over the Constitutions of Clarendon, where Henry aimed to restrict the power of the church and the Pope while reforming civil law. One in six people in the country were lay clergymen, not priests, but could claim 'benefit of clergy' and be tried in a church court for any crimes – where they would usually receive a much lighter sentence than if they'd been tried in a civil court. Henry wanted these 'criminous clerks' to be tried in a civil court, which he saw as restoring order after the civil war between Stephen and Matilda. He proposed a solution that if a church court convicted someone of murder, the criminal should be deprived of the church's protection and the punishment should be set by the civil court. Becket saw this as undermining the whole concept of clerical immunity – once someone was handed over to the civil courts, he was effectively no longer a clerk.

At Clarendon, Becket told his bishops that they had to sign Henry's proposals – but Becket himself then dressed as a penitent, sentenced himself to a fast and repented of the oath. Becket's letters say that he told the bishops to sign so that Henry's wrath would be diverted from them – but he intended to continue opposing the proposals himself.

In 1164 Henry summoned Becket to a trial at Northampton, accusing him of embezzling £300 while he was Lord Chancellor. Becket denied the charges but wanted the matter settled quickly so he offered to pay the £300. Henry accused him of treason, and Becket said that the court had no right to judge him because he was a clerk. Becket left for France, where he thought he'd be safe. Henry promptly sequestered all his property and issued edicts against his supporters.

Becket publicly excommunicated de Broc, and had almost persuaded the Pope to excommunicate Henry; and then Henry got the Archbishop of York to crown Henry the Young King (Henry II's second son). Coronations were a right of the Archbishop of Canterbury, and Becket was furious. He agreed a compromise with the king that he would return to England and re-crown Henry the Younger – but the prince refused to meet Becket (despite the fact that Becket had also looked after the prince in his own home – it was the custom at the time that the children of noble houses were fostered out to other nobles – and at one point Henry the Younger was closer to Becket than he was to his own father).

Becket began excommunicating everyone who had opposed him – including the Archbishop of York and the bishops of London and Salisbury. Henry, at the winter court in Normandy, was furious, and demanded to know who would rid him of this troublesome priest. It was probably a cry of frustration, but the king's words were taken as a royal command. So four of his knights – Reginald Fitzurse, Hugh de Moreville, William de Tracy and Richard le Bret – travelled back to England. So the story goes, they discussed the murder with de Broc by candlelight at Saltwood. And then the four knights (without de Broc) rode to Canterbury Cathedral. They met Becket and demanded that he should go back to France with them and account to the King for his actions. Becket refused. The next day, 29 December 1170, they tried to drag him out of the cathedral, and he resisted. The knights struck him with their swords – also severely injuring Edward Grim, a visiting monk from

Cambridge who tried to protect Becket and later wrote an eyewitness account of the event. However, Becket stood firm; at the next blow he fell to his knees, saying, 'For the name of Jesus and the protection of the Church, I am ready to embrace death.' Le Bret thrust his sword so hard through Becket's head that the sword broke on the cathedral floor – and rather grusomely, according to Grim, '[Becket's] crown, which was large, separated from his head so that the blood turned white from the brain yet no less did the brain turn red from the blood; it purpled the appearance of the church with the colours of the lily and the rose.'

Becket – who was wearing a hair shirt underneath his habits – had become a martyr.

The pope excommunicated the four knights and banned Henry from taking mass until he'd made reparation for his sin. Three years after his death, Becket was canonised, and Henry II made public penance at Becket's tomb, the following year. Becket's tomb became the most popular pilgrimage site in England; but the problem of 'criminous clerks' continued until the Reformation.

Hugh Bigod and the end of the castle

In 1173, Hugh joined Henry II's sons, Henry and Robert, the Earl of Leicester, in a rebellion against the king. Their army of Flemish mercenaries had been repulsed by Dunwich (see page 51), but had landed at Walton. They attacked the castles at Walton and Orford (see pages 67 and 125, respectively) but failed; but they regrouped at Framlingham, adding more supporters on the way, and on 13 October 1173 the rebel army arrived at Haughley, 10,000 strong.

De Broc, by contrast, had a tiny garrison – according to some sources, he had only 30 knights. He didn't stand a chance of standing against the rebels. The attack lasted for just one afternoon; de Broc surrendered, and some of the knights were taken prison for the ransom money. Bodies were piled high – according to local legend, they were buried in nearby Hall Gardens – and the castle was left burning while Bigod and his men marched to the castle at Eye (see page 59).

Henry II ordered the destruction of Haughley after the rebellion had ended, although John Kirby's *The Suffolk Traveller* (written in 1744) says that the castle was rebuilt by the Ufford family and, even though the castle was abandoned in 1416 and left to fall into ruins, Kirby said that he could still see a square bailey there, with ramparts and a moat and a circular keep.

Nowadays, the only remains to be seen of the castle are the ramparts, earthwork and moat.

Secret tunnels

Haughley House, sited just outside the bailey, is meant to have two secret tunnels, now sealed up; one of them supposedly leads to the church.

Priory of St Olaves, Herringfleet

The priory of St Olaves in Herringfleet (OS grid reference TM 45869953) is the remains of a 13th-century Augustinian priory. It is in the care of English The beginnings of the priory

Herringfleet priory. Photograph by author.

The priory was founded around 1216 by Roger FitzOsbert near the ancient ferry of St Olaves. The original dedication was to St Olave, the Blessed Virgin Mary and St Edmund, king and martyr. This is the only dedication to St Olave in Suffolk (apart from the now demolished church of Creeting St Olave).

St Olaf was the son of a Norwegian jarl; he became king of Norway in 1016 and, after being christened, proceeded to Christianise Norway. However, as he was a warrior king, his form of Christianisation was that his subject should either accept the new religion or be beheaded! In 1225 the priory was granted the right to hold an annual fair on St Olaf's Day, 29 July.

Originally the area of the priory within the walls was about 10 acres; however, after dissolution, the priory was partially demolished and the stone used for buildings elsewhere in the village. The church was about 74 feet long and tiles have been discovered in the ruins to suggest that the floor was originally in black and yellow chequerwork. The cloister was 68 feet square, with a 10-foot-wide perimeter path; and the refectory is very unusual because it is one of the few buildings made of brick in the 14th century.

Herringfleet priory refectory undercroft. Photograph by author.

Scandals

In 1493 the priory had a visitation by the Norwich dioceses. They were visited by Archdeacon Nicholas Goldwell, the bishop's deputy, on 30 January. He examined Thomas Bagot, the prior, and the five canons separately and there were three main complaints: that William Cokke, one of the priors, was bad-tempered and quarrelsome; that the prior didn't show the accounts of the house to the canons; and that there wasn't enough to eat, so the canons were starving.

The next visitation was held in July 1514. The prior, William Dale, told Bishop Nix that he showed the senior canons the yearly accounts, and the canons were obedient. The sub-prior, Robert Starys, said that they always started mattins late, they only sang offices on festivals and Sunday, and despite the fact that the prior had increased their lands by 25%, the house was still very poor and the canons didn't have enough to live on. The bishop said that they had to observe complete silence in cloister and choir on Fridays, but otherwise all was well.

The final three visitations showed the priory was poor but 'omnia bene'.

Dissolution

The priory was suppressed on 3 February 1536/7. Legh and Leyton made their usual report of scandals before the suppression, but the commissioners – Sir

Humfrey Wyngefeld, Richard Southwell, and Thomas Myldemay – ignored it and gave William Dale, the prior, a pension of 10 marks.

After Dissolution

The site was granted to Sir Henry Jerningham; in 1547 he built a three-storey mansion near the cloisters, using the monastic remains. The mansion was demolished in 1784 and the stone was used for local buildings, the bridge and for surfacing the road. In 1823, more stone was taken from the ruins to repair the church at Herringfleet. Two years, later, the undercroft was converted into a cottage; it continued to be used as a cottage until 1902.

Dr W. Arnold Smith Wynne, deputy surgeon-general of the Indian Army, retired to St Olaves and lived near the priory. He wrote a monograph on the priory in 1914, where he says that he spoke to Mrs Baird, who was born in the priory in 1826, when she was almost 80; she told him that she could remember half a dozen skeletons being unearthed in the garden when she was a child. The estate thatcher added that when he was working in the garden in about 1845, he discovered a 'clay coffin' which contained a human skeleton.

Wynne started excavating the priory in 1904, with the help of his gardener, his waterman and a retired soldier. He found a Roman mill stone used as the base of the central column in the east part of the refectory undercroft; and in his account of the excavations he admits that in 1883 he removed various stones from a field which he realised years later were priory outbuildings, but as he didn't recognise what they were at the time, he didn't make any notes about their position.

Secret tunnels

One story which often seems to be involved with monastic buildings is the 'secret tunnel' that opens up, and the brave man who explores it while playing a fiddle (see Bury St Edmunds, page 36). Herringfleet is no exception. Dr Smith Wynne says that the last occupant of Crypt Cottage told him that the tunnel led from the entrance of the priory to Burgh Castle – and the last man to go down the tunnel, playing the fiddle, never came back! According to Dr Smith Wynne, the tunnel did indeed exist – but it was simply a vaulted passage, and he filled it in to stop the floor of the crypt falling in.

Zodiac signs

Dr Smith Wynne's monograph also speaks about strange stones found on the piers of the bridge that was pulled down in 1847. Apparently, in the stones below the low water mark, there were markings of zodiac signs; he said that six of the stones were rescued, and he believed that they'd come from the priory.

Hoxne Priory

Hoxne Priory (OS grid reference TM 183 764) is the remains of a Benedictine priory at Abbey Farm, located near the centre of the village of Hoxne. The remains include a stretch of wall about 40 metres long, which is incorporated in the building of the farmhouse, and part of a moat. The farm is in private hands and there is no access to the public.

The Beginnings of the Priory

A secular college dedicated to St Aethelberht was founded here at some point before 951, but it was destroyed soon after it was built. The site then became a secular cathedral in 1040, when Hoxne was a joint see with North Elmham. The church of St Peter and the Chapel of St Edmund, King and Martyr were granted to the monks of Norwich Cathedral Priory in 1101, and the stone priory was built on the site of the wooden chapel, where St Edmund's body rested for 33 years until it was taken to Bury St Edmunds in 903. According to the 18th-century historian Francis Blomefield, monks moved into the building around 1226 and the priory was completed in around 1267; at this point the priory churchyard was consecrated by the Bishop of Norwich, Roger de Skerning. Six or seven monks lived there, under a prior who was appointed by the prior of Norwich; they also set up a school for the children of the parish.

Figure of St Edmund from village hall, Hoxne. Photograph by author.

The Ending of the Priory

William Castleton was the last prior; he could see what was happening with the dissolution of the monasteries, so he sold the property to Sir Richard Gresham and sent the monks back to Norwich. The King pardoned him for this and ratified the transfer in 1538, and the priory was dissolved. The site later passed to the Maynard family, who built an Italianate house on the site (now called 'Abbey Farm').

The Martyrdom of St Edmund

When Edmund's forces were overrun by the Danes, Edmund regrouped at Hegelisdun. Since 1101 this has been associated with Hoxne, whose claim to be the site of martyrdom was first noted in the foundation charter of Norwich Cathedral Priory.

So the story goes, that evening at Hoxne, Edmund hid under Goldbrook Bridge. However, he was wearing gilt spurs, and the moon reflected them on the water. A newly married couple came across the bridge, saw the reflection of his spurs in the water, and betrayed him to the Danes. In response, Edmund is said to have pronounced a curse upon any couple who crossed the bridge on their way to the church to get married – and since that date it's said that brides and grooms refuse to cross that bridge on their wedding day, even if they have to go out of their way, because they feel that crossing the bridge would be unlucky.

When the current bridge was built in 1878, excavations discovered spear heads, knives and stirrups.

Plaque from village hall, Hoxne, showing St Edmund hiding from the Danes and the wedding party. Photograph by author.

Goldbrook Bridge, Hoxne. Photograph by author.

According to Abbo of Fleury, once the Danes had captured Edmund, they whipped him, and then tied him to a tree and shot him with arrows 'until he bristled with them like a hedgehog or thistle'.

Then Edmund's head was cut off and his head was thrown into bramble thickets in the wood. His body was soon found and taken back to Hoxne, but Edmund's supporters couldn't find his head. According to the poet John Lydgate, writing at the Abbey of Bury St Edmunds in the early 15th century, about 40

Wall painting from St Mary's church in Troston, Suffolk, showing St Edmund being struck with arrows by the Danes. Photograph by author.

days after Edmund's death his friends split up into small groups to explore the wood. Some of them got lost and cried out, 'Where are you?' They were answered – not by their friends, but by Edmund's head, which replied, 'Here! Here! Here!'

They went to the spot where they'd heard the voice, and were surprised to find a wolf there, holding Edmund's head between his front paws.

Bench end from the church of St Peter and St Paul, Hoxne, showing Edmund's head between the paws of a wolf. Photograph by author.

The wolf let them take Edmund's head and carry it back to where his body lay; the moment that Edmund's head was reunited with his body, the flesh became one and the only sign that he had ever been beheaded was by a very narrow red line round his throat.

The wolf followed Edmund's men and attended the funeral, then went back to living in the wood.

Edmund's men built a wooden chapel over his grave and his body rested there for 30 years, until it was formally translated (moved) to Bury St Edmunds – where Edmund's story continues (see page 25).

Edmund's oak and the healing spring

The site of the priory, there is a spring; it's said that the spring emerged on the spot where Edmund's head was found between the wolf's paws. It was known as a healing spring in the Middle Ages.

In 1854, Lord Hervey addressed the members of the Archaeological Institute when they visited Bury St Edmund's:

> I cannot help adverting into a most singular tradition, to which I confess I give implicit credence. At Hoxne, a few miles from hence, was an old oak tree, which had always been known as St Edmund's Oak. The common tradition was (perhaps it had ceased to be the common belief) that it was the very identical oak to which King Edmund was tied, some thousand years ago, when he was shot at by the Danes. Some seven or eight years since, this venerable tree split from extreme old age, and in its very centre, which was then exposed to view, was found an old arrow-head. This remarkable fact, coupled with the previous tradition, makes me believe that this was the very oak tree to which St Edmund was bound in the forest of Hoxne.

There is a stone monument which marks the spot where the tree grew. So was it the spot where Edmund was martyred? Although the tradition is very romantic, it seems that the 'arrowhead' turned out to be a piece of bent wire – so maybe not. Though when the tree was cut and the rings were counted, it was said that the tree was a thousand years old; and a piece of it was kept in the church for many years.

Monument marking the spot of the tree where St Edmund was killed, Hoxne. Photograph by author. Monument plinth reads: St Edmund the Martyr, AD 870. Oak Tree fell August 1848 by its own weight.

The Hoxne treasure

On 16 November 1992, Eric Lawes was a metal-detecting in a field, looking for a hammer, when he discovered something that he recognised as being very unusual. Sensibly, rather than digging up his find, he reported it to the Suffolk Archaeological Unit, who were able to excavate it. It turned out to be the largest hoard of 4th- and 5th-century Roman gold and silver ever found in the United Kingdom. They had been buried in a wooden chest; only the iron fittings of the chest survived. Inside were silver locks from smaller caskets; there were also traces of cloth and hay, which had been wrapped round some of the objects.

The entire hoard was declared treasure trove on 2 September 1993, and the hoard was bought by the British Musuem. Mr Lawes and the farmer in whose field the hoard was discovered received £1.75 millon, and split the money equally between them. In a poll following the 2003 BBC television documentary *Our Top Ten Treasures*, the Hoxne hoard was voted the third most important treasure unearthed in Britain.

The treasure included 14,780 coins: 565 gold, 14,191 silver, and 24 bronze. Most of the gold coins (*solidi*) were struck between 394 and 405, dating from the reign of Honorius and Arcadius. The silver coins (*siliquae*) were minted between 358 and 408, covering the reign of fifteen different emperors; many had been clipped around the edges.

As well as the coins, there were 200 pieces of gold jewellery and silver tableware. The jewellery included rings, necklaces and a gold chain that was worn over the shoulders and under the arms, joined at the front and back by decorative brooches. There were nineteen bracelets; some had figures of animals and others had geometric patterns. One included a dedication to the woman who wore it: *UTERE FELIX DOMINA IULIANE* , basically wishing Lady Juliana good luck.

The tableware included 78 spoons (some of which had inscriptions of the owner's name, Aurelius Ursicinus), 20 ladles and some smaller objects, including four extremely rare pepperpots or *piperatoria* (one of which is shaped as an empress and contains a disk with three sorts of openings so the pot could be kept closed, filled with pepper, or used to sprinkle the spice on food) and a silver tigress that's thought to be a handle from a large vase.

There were also beauty accessories, including a pair shaped like ibises with a toothpick at one end and a scoop at the other end which might have been used for cleaning ears or taking cosmetics from small bowls. Others have a scoop at one end and a socket at the other, so they might have been brushes.

Ipswich Castle

Given that the history of the town of Ipswich can be traced back to Saxon times, and its importance as a port, it would be very surprising if a castle had not existed in the town.

We do not know exactly when the castle was built or where it was sited – but we do know that the castle was occupied by Hugh Bigod during the period of King Stephen's reign, and that the castle was besieged by Stephen's army in 1153 and was captured.

Some sources think that the castle was demolished then on Stephen's orders; others think that demolition took place in 1176, because in 1173 the Earl of Leicester and his Flemings landed at Walton (see page 67), then marched to Ipswich and captured the castle there before attacking Haughley (see page 83).

The battle of Fornham St Genevieve

The Earl of Leicester and Hugh Bigod's forces, fresh from conquering Haughley, intended to march to Leicester and relieve it from the royal siege. However, royalist troops had mustered at Bury St Edmunds under the leadership of the chief justiciar, Richard de Lucy, along with the constable, Humphrey de Bohun; the earls of Gloucester, Cornwall and Arundel; and Hugh Bigod's son, Roger, who carried the standard of St Edmund for the royalists.

On 16 October 1173, the opposing armies met at Fornham St Genevieve. Arundel called out, 'Let us attack them for the honour of God and St Edmund!' The Flemings were routed; many drowned, others were trampled under hooves, and those who tried to escape over the marshes were followed by the locals – who'd joined the battle, wanting revenge for the way the Flemings had pillaged their homes. The Countess of Leicester was captured; according to the monastic chronicler Matthew Paris, the Countess of Leicester threw away her ring top stop it falling into enemy hands, and a ruby and gold ring was found at Fornham in the early 1800s which is thought to have been her ring. Jordan Fantosme, who was one of de Lucy's men, told the story of the battle in a poem and says that Petronelle, the Countess of Leicester, tried to run away and fell in a ditch, where she lost her ring. According to Fantosme, Petronelle tried to drown herself rather than give herself up to the enemy, but Simon de Vahull (one of the royalists) rescued her.

The Earl of Leicester managed to reach the church at Fornham St Genevieve but was defeated and, together with his wife, was taken to Bury and handed over to Henry II.

Human bones and fragments of weapons have been found near the battle site, along with pennies dating from the reign of Henry II. The 19th-century academic

John Rokewood edited Jocelin de Brakelond's *Chronicle*, which gives an account of the battle, and added a note:

> In felling, in 1826, an ancient pollard ash that stood upon a low mound of earth about 15 feet in diameter, near the church of Fornham St Genevieve, a heap of skeletons, not less than 40, were discovered, in good preservation, piled in order, tier upon tier, with their faces upwards and their feet pointing to the centre. Several of the skulls exhibited evident marks of violence, as if they had been pierced with arrows, or cleft with a sword.

These remains have since vanished, but in 2008, when the river was being dredged, workmen discovered a skull that had been pierced by a spear or iron arrow, along with other bones. Experts identified the remains as being at least medieval, so it could be that they belonged to one of the Flemish army.

The site of the castle

Whenever Ipswich Castle was dismantled, as John Kirby stated in 1735, it was 'so entirely demolished, that not the least Rubbish of it is to be found' – which makes it difficult to work out exactly where the castle was sited.

Although there is a place in Ipswich called Castle Hill, it's more likely that the 'castle' there was actually a Roman villa. The historian Norman Scarfe suggested that Ipswich Castle was sited by the Henley Road; but historian Robert Malster thinks it is more likely to be in the area near the Cornhill, because Elm Street does not fit the rest of the 'grid pattern' of the streets of Ipswich, and it's possible that the curve of the street follows the line of the bailey. Malster also says that the area was known as 'the Mount' and any castle sited there would control the main entrance to Ipswich from both Bury St Edmunds and Norwich.

The Priories of Ipswich

During medieval times there were two priories and three friaries in Ipswich. The first that we know to have been set up was the Holy Trinity Priory, an Augustinian foundation, in 1177; the Priory of St Peter and St Paul, also an Augustinian foundation, was set up some time towards the end of the reign of Henry II, in the late 1180s. Greyfriars Priory was founded at some time before 1236, Blackfriars Priory was founded in 1263 and Whitefriars was founded in 1278.

Ipswich Holy Trinity Priory

Although the Domesday book mentions a Holy Trinity church in Ipswich, the priory was not established until 1177. According to the historian Leland, the founder was Normanius Gastrode, son of Egnostri. The priory burned down in its early years and was rebuilt in 1194 by John de Oxford, Bishop of Norwich. Originally there were only seven canons and a prior, but as the house grew richer the numbers increased to about 20.

Scandals

In 1393 there was a serious incident at the priory; John Bendel, one of the canons, was granted a royal pardon for causing the death of Godfrey Neketon, the cook.

There was a visitation held by Bishop Nix in August 1514; there were complaints by the canons that the servants were really insolent. The Bishop took it seriously enough that the servants' words were actually recorded in English – the rest of the visitation report was made in Latin. According to the visitation, two of the servants said: 'Yf soo be that ye medyll with me I shall gyff the such a strippe that thou shallt not recover yt a twelvemonyth after.'

At the next visitation in June 1526, Thomas Whighte, the prior, complained that John Carver was disobedient. Canon Thomas Edgore said that the prior didn't render annual accounts, and John Shribbs said that the prior didn't have much control over the canons, who could confess to whom they liked, go out of the priory precincts without asking for permission, and be as excessive as they wished. The bishop gave them quite a long list of injunctions. He told Carver that he had to obey the prior, or he would be thrown into prison; he told the prior that he to make the annual accounts and appoint a confessor; and all the canons had to observe silence properly and only leave the precincts with permission from the prior.

In June 1532, the canons complained that the cook was dirty and the food and cooking were bad, and the prior still didn't produce annual accounts. The bishop issued injunctions to remedy the problems.

The end of the Holy Trinity Priory

The priory was suppressed on 9 February, 1536/7, and the last prior, John Thetford (alias Colyn), was given a pension of £15. The site was granted to Sir Humphrey Wingfield and Sir Thomas Rushe.

The priory was demolished by 1548, and Edward Wythypoll began building Christchurch Mansion on the site. The building was damaged by fire in the 17th century and rebuilt. In 1895, when the house and park came up for sale, brewing magnate Felix Cobbold bought the house and gave it to the town on condition that

Christchurch mansion, Ipswich. Photograph by author.

Christchurch mansion; plate from Thomas Kitson Cromwell's Excursions Through Suffolk, *1818-9. Photograph by author.*

they bought the park. The house then became a museum, and the park was opened to the public on 11 April 1895.

The Ghosts of Christchurch and the Secret Room

There are meant to be three sets of ghosts that haunt Christchurch Mansion. The first is of a woman in Edwardian dress, who holds the hand of two children and dances round and laughs; the second is a servant girl who died in unexplained circumstances; and the third is a grey lady.

There's also an 'alcove room' in the house which was once concealed by sliding panel; the only way to get to it was to use the door of the closet beneath it as a step. It was probably a Catholic hiding place.

The Martyrs of Ipswich

In Christchurch Park there is a monument to nine Protestant martyrs who were burned on the Cornhill – the square in front of Ipswich town hall – between 1555 and 1558. The memorial was unveiled in December 1903 by the Dean of Canterbury, and the names of the martyrs are engraved on its stone base. It was paid for by a private subscription which was opened in November 1902 after the journalist Nina Frances Layard told the story of the martyrs in a series of articles in the *East Anglian Daily Times* between 1898 and 1902.

The inscription on the monument reads:

Memorial to the martyrs in Christchurch Park, Ipswich. Photograph by author.

This monument is erected to the memory of nine Ipswich martyrs who for their constancy to the Protestant faith suffered death by burning.

Oh may Thy soldiers, faithful, true and bold,
Fight as the saints who nobly fought of old,
And win with them the victor's crown of gold.
Alleluia.

Alexander Gooch of Woodbridge was a weaver who refused to admit that the Pope was the supreme head of the church and also refused to receive Mass. He had to go into hiding and was pursued by Justice Noone. Alice Driver was the daughter of a ploughman who had obtained a Bible written in English and came to believe that the way that Mass was celebrated in the Roman Catholic Church was idolatrous; when she stopped going to church, she too received the attention of Justice Noone.

Gooch was hiding in Alice Driver's house when they heard that Justice Noone and his men were coming in search of them. They hid in a haystack, but Noone's men stuck pitchforks through the hay and discovered them. They were taken first to jail in Melton, and then to Bury Assizes.

Alice Driver was incredibly courageous; even though Sir Clement Heigham, the MP for Ipswich and the Speaker of the House of Commons, ordered that her ears should be cut off, she wasn't cowed. During the inquisition, the Chancellor of Norwich asked her why she had been imprisoned, she told him that he knew as well as she did. When he said he didn't know, she replied, 'Then have ye done much wrong thus to imprison me, and know no cause why; for I know no evil that I have done, I thank God, and I hope there is no man that can accuse me of any notorious fact that I have done, justly.'

She clearly ran rings round the Chancellor; her last statement was, 'Have you any more to say? God be honoured. You be not able to resist the Spirit of God in me, a poor woman. I am an honest poor man's daughter, never brought up in the University, as you have been, but I have driven the plough before my father many a time (I thank God): yet, notwithstanding, in the defence of God's truth, and in the cause of my Master Christ, by His grace I will set my foot against the foot of any of you all, in the maintenance and defence of the same, and if I had a thousand lives, they should go for payment thereof.'

Alice Driver and Gooch were both condemned and sentenced to be burned in Ipswich. At 7 a.m. on 4 November 1558, they were taken to the stake and knelt down to say their prayers. The sheriff, Sir Henry Dowell, said that they should be chained to the stake; when the heavy chain was passed around Alice's neck, she said, 'Oh! Here is a goodly neckerchief; blessed be God for it.' People in the crowd started coming up to the two martyrs and shaking their hand; when the sheriff ordered the arrest, even more people came to shake their hands and the sheriff had to give in.

And then the broom was lit and the martyrs were executed.

Ipswich Priory of St Peter and St Paul

Not much is known about the priory of St Peter and St Paul, which used to stand next to the church of St Peter and covered an area of about 6 acres by the time of dissolution. It's thought that it was founded towards the end of the reign of Henry II by ancestors of Thomas de Lacy and his wife Alice (who gave it lands in Duxford in 1344).

St Peter's church, Ipswich. Photograph by author.

The bishop's visitations seem to have gone reasonably well; in 1514, Prior Godwyn and canon John Laurence complained to the vicar-general (who did the visitation on behave of Bishop Nix) that the monks did not get up for mattins, and other canons complained that there was no schoolmaster and no breakfast (*jentacula*) in the morning. The vicar-general ruled that the canons had to get up for mattins, the prior had to find a grammar teacher for the canons, and the prior had to find a chest with three locks so the priory seal was kept safe.

The priory of St Peter and St Paul was suppressed in May 1528; as with many of the small Suffolk priories, their revenues were meant to go towards the founding of Cardinal's College in Ipswich (see below). As Wolsey's college was built on the site of the priory, its buildings served as the college deanery. However, after Wolsey's fall from grace, building was halted and the college was shut. The King granted the site to Thomas Alvard, one of his ushers.

In 1823, a letter to *Gentlemen's Magazine* stated that some workmen, who were putting a drain across the garden of what was once Wolsey's College, discovered the crypt of the priory; it was 8 feet below the garden and was 5.5 feet wide. Many bones were found while digging the drain.

Blackfriars Friary

Blackfriars Friary (OS grid reference TM 160 442) was a Dominican friary; it was founded in 1263 by Henry III. He bought the original site from Hugh, the son of Gerard de Langeston, and in 1263 he bought the property next door and gave it to the Friary. The site was expanded several times over the next hundred years, sometimes with permission – and sometimes without! In February 1348 the town bailiffs granted the friars a plot of land, on condition that they maintained the town walls opposite the plot and the townspeople could use their gates in times of necessity. At one point the site of the priory covered the area between Foundation Street, Star Lane, and the town ditch and bank that ran parallel to Lower Brook Street.

The Friary was dissolved in November 1538 by the Bishop of Dover; one of the king's serjeant-at-arms, William Aubyn, became the tenant of the site. After dissolution, the buildings were used as the Bridewell, shire hall and grammar school. The buildings were pulled down in 1852, though the remains of St Mary's Church can still be seen on the corner of Foundation Street.

The remains of Blackfriars Friary, Ipswich. Photograph by author.

The Ghosts of Blackfriars

There is meant to be a Black Friar who haunts the site; he hovers above the ground and either points at or pokes people.

Tooley's Almshouses in Foundation Street were set up in 1551 by Henry Tooley; today it is still a charitable retirement home. It's said that sometimes the ghost of a lady is seen sitting, sewing, in the oldest block; allegedly soon after she is seen, one of the residents dies.

Greyfriars Friary

Greyfriars Friary (OS grid reference TM 1609 4430) was a Franciscan friary; it founded before 1236 by Sir Robert Tiptot, of Nettlestead, and his wife Una. The monks were very poor and the friary had no lands, just the site and gardens. On 1 April 1538, Lord Wentworth of Nettlestead wrote to Cromwell about the poverty of the priory and complained that they were selling the plate. As Wentworth claimed that he was related to the founder, he sent for the warden and asked for an explanation; the warden said that they'd gathered only £5 in the last 12 months and needed to find the money from somewhere, so he'd sold the priory silver. Then

Wentworth came to the real point of his letter: he asked Cromwell to grant the friary site to him.

Cromwell's reply was to send his special friary visitor, Richard Ingworth, to Ipswich on 7 April. Ingworth drew up an inventory; leaving the priory just the bare essentials, he took the remainder and locked it up at Blackfriars in a 'close house'. Then he found the plate that had been sold or pledged and recovered it – including from Wentworth. The inventory documented everything in the church, the kitchen, the buttery, the garner, the cheese house, the warden's chambers, and (unusually) the vice-warden's chamber.

The friary was dissolved in 1538. Remains of the precinct wall and several graves from the cemetery have been excavated.

PJ McGinty's, Ipswich. Photograph by author.

The Ghost at PJ Mcginty's

PJ Mcinty's pub in Northgate Street is thought to be haunted by a monk from Greyfriars who was murdered and thrown down the well. Allegedly, a beating heart has been heard in the basement.

Secret Tunnels

There's meant to be a secret passage from Stoke Hall to the site of Greyfriars Priory. This may however be linked to the wine cellars that Thomas Cartwright excavated under the stables in 1740, which were 180 feet long in total; they were left in situ when the buildings were demolished, and were used as air raid shelters during the Second World War.

There are also meant to be tunnels which link Christchurch Mansion and a wine merchant's cellars on Fore Street, as well as the Custom House, Ancient House and the site of Holywell's Manor.

Carmelite Friary

The Carmelite (Whitefriars) friary was established in 1278 by Sir Thomas de Loudham.They were based on the south side of the Butter Market (now a shopping precinct) and by Dissolution their land stretched from St Stephen's Street to Queen

Street. The friary itself must have been quite large, as it was used for meetings of provincial chapters. Several very literary monks and noted scholars came from the friary, including friar Richard Lavingham who died 1383 and wrote 90 books.

As with the Greyfriars, they were suppressed in November 1538 by Richard Ingworth, the Bishop of Dover. The site was granted to Charles Lambard.

Ghosts

Before the Buttermarket Centre was built, it was the site of W. S. Cowell's engineering factory. It's said that several employees saw a monk in the area, and phantom footsteps were heard in the factory. It's also said that moving shadows have been seen in the underground car park of the Buttermarket Centre.

The Buttermarket Centre, Ipswich. Photograph by author.

Wolsey's College

Thomas Wolsey was born in Ipswich in 1475, the son of a merchant, though some sources claim he was a butcher's son. He went to Magdalen College in Oxford and was ordained in 1498. He became chaplain to the Archbishop of Canterbury and then to Henry VII, winning a reputation as an efficient administrator. He became archbishop of York in 1509 and the pope made him a cardinal, the following year; and Henry VIII made him Lord Chancellor in 1515.

At the peak of his power, he formed a grand ambition – to found a college at Oxford, plus a feeder school (or college) in each diocese, starting with his home town of Ipswich. To this end, he had permission from the king to suppress many of the small monasteries and use their revenues to build his college. At Oxford, he founded Cardinal's College (later called King's College, and now Christ Church). In Ipswich, he decided to build his college on the site of St Peter's Priory. He planned to have a dean, 12 priests, 8 clerks, 8 singing boys and poor scholars plus a grammar teacher, and 13 poor men; all would pray for the king, Wolsey, and the souls of Wolsey's parents.

The pedestrian gateway to Wolsey's college, Ipswich. Photograph by author.

Building began in 1528 and Wolsey asked Elizabeth, the Dowager Countess of Oxford (the widow of John de Vere) if he could take stone from her cliff at Harwich. She refused, saying that it would endanger the town; Wolsey was displeased and wrote to her on 15 July 1528, accusing her of refusing just because she didn't want him to have the stone. She replied, saying, 'Be it hurtful or otherwise, your grace to do your pleasure.' The higher Wolsey's star rose, the haughtier he became – and the more unpopular.

Not all the stone for the college came from Harwich, because Wolsey also had permission from French king to take stone from quarry at Caen. On 26 September 1528, William Capon, the dean of the college, wrote to Wolsey saying that he had 120 tons of Caen stone, 100 tons more were to come after Michaelmas and 1,000 more before Easter – so clearly Wolsey was planning a huge building.

The foundation stone of the college was found 1789 as part of a wall in Woulfoun's Lane; it was given to Christ Church, Oxford. The foundation stone is inscribed '*Anno Christi 1528, et regni Henrici Octavi Regis Angliae 20 mensis vero Junii 15, positum per Johannem Episcopum Lidensem*' (i.e. it was laid by John Holte, the bishop of Lydda (in the Holy Land). Holte also the laid first stone at Wolsey's college in Oxford.)

However, Wolsey's star was starting to fade; he became the scapegoat for Henry VIII's failure to obtain a divorce from Katherine, his foreign policy was failing badly, and in October 1529 he was deprived of office. A year later, he was arraigned for treason, and Henry VIII claimed Wolsey's property. The commissioners made an inventory of the college at Ipswich on 14 November 1530; they seized treasure, stripped the buildings, and then accused the dean of keeping £1,000 of the cardinal's treasure. Dean Capon denied it, but the commissioners didn't believe him and waited at the college for 5 days (with 6 yeomen of the guard and 18 others). On 21 November, the Duke of Norfolk's council took possession of the buildings, and on 22 November, Capon left for London. A week later, Wolsey died at Leicester on the way to his trial. And in 1531 1,300 tons of stone and 600 tons of flint were taken from the college to Westminster. The only remains of the college is a small brick gate on College Street.

According to the 19th-century historian John Wodderspoon, the area then became the 'spot for depositing of the refuse and filth of the town'.

The Witch of Ipswich

Mary Lakeland (or Lackland) was burnt at the stake on 9 September 1645; she confessed to having been a witch for more than 20 years. A contemporary pamphlet, *The Lawes against Witches and Conjurration*, says that she was given three imps, in the form of a mole and two little dogs. She bewitched her husband John; then sent one dog to Mr Lawrence 'to torment him and take away his life' and the other to do the same for his child, because he'd asked her for 12 shillings she owed him. She also sent a mole to Mrs Jennings' maid Sarah Clark, to do the same job as the dogs to the Lawrences, because the maid wouldn't lend her a needle or repay the shilling she owed Mary. She sent an imp to Mr Beale, who taught her grand-daughter and refused to 'have' (i.e. marry) Mary after her husband's death – and at the time of the trial, Beale was living in torment, with half his body rotting away.

Mary was sentenced to being burned at the stake: not for witchcraft, but for murdering her husband. But the witchcraft rumours persisted; after her death a piece of flesh that had grown on Beales' thigh 'after the form of a dog' broke off, and his illnesses began to be cured, including a huge running sore.

Allegedly, in 1997, a shop in the Ancient House began to be haunted. Flower displays were moved, car park tickets vanished and reappeared the following day, drinks disappeared, doors stuck and people were tapped on the shoulder when nobody was nearby. A cabinet key disappeared – and while it was still locked, items within it were moved (as the original positions could be seen in the dust). The manager called in a medium, who said that she kept getting the name 'Lakeland' – the shop was Lakeland Plastics.

It turned out that Mary Lakeland's husband, John, was a barber (i.e. acted as a surgeon and a dentist) and they'd lived next door to Ancient House, then lived in by the Royalist Sparrowe family. So was that why she haunted the Ancient House – because she too had been a royalist? Local historian Pete Jennings believes that she was a royalist supporter who was accused of being a witch and executed for her political beliefs; there was no evidence against her, so the politicians in Ipswich didn't want to send her to Bury for trial. The quickest way to get rid of her was to accuse her of murdering her husband by witchcraft – and the penalty for murdering a husband meant being burned at the stake.

Ancient House, Ipswich. Photograph by author.

Granville Squires, writing in 1934, says that in 1801, when a workman cut into the wall of the Ancient House so he could reach the underside of the roof tiles, he discovered a long garret with ornamented beams; it was a chapel which extended from floor below, but a floor was put in so that the lower half could be used as a normal room and the top half used in secret as a Catholic chapel. The window of the garret is invisible from anywhere outside, and wooden angels were found there. There was also a tradition that Charles II took refuge there, though there's no evidence for this.

Ixworth Priory

The Priory of Ixworth was an Augustine priory dedicated to St Mary; the remains – cloister ranges, which are incorporated in a Georgian manor house built on the site – are not open to the public.

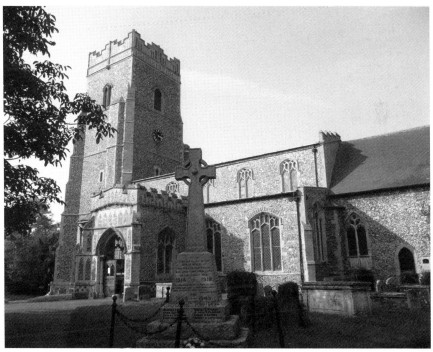

St Mary's church, Ixworth. Photograph by author.

Beginnings of the priory

The priory was founded by Gilbert le Blunt in about 1100, on a site near the church. It was destroyed during a riot at some point in the middle of the century, and was rebuilt by his son William in 1170 on a slightly different site.

Scandals

In 1361, Thomas de Ellingham left Thremhall Priory in Essex without permission, and became an apostate (i.e. resigned his faith) for two years. Then he joined Ixworth Priory, without telling them about his past; he was ordained again and made subdeacon.

The prior was in trouble in 1283, and two justices were sent to make an enquiry. William, the prior, along with John the cellarer, were accused of assaulting Ralph de Bonevill, the serjeant of Otto de Grandison and Peter de Chaumpvent at Ixworth, and of stealing goods while Otto and Peter were with the king in Wales.

Most of the bishop's visitations, however, showed no problems. In 1514, when Bishop Nix visited, there were some minor complaints: that the chamberlain, John Bache, was a layman rather than a monk; they didn't have a tailor to make their clothes; the clock didn't work; and the sacrist didn't light all the lamps properly. The bishop's injunctions meant that the problems should have been corrected – and the report at the next visitation was 'omnia bene' – but the tailoring problem recurred in 1526, along with an insolent butler and the prior giving farm tenancies without the monks' consent.

Legh and Leyton tried to make their usual reports of scandal, just before Dissolution, but could only force one of the eighteen monks to confess to incontinence (impurity); instead, they claimed that there was a conspiracy of silence.

Dissolution

The priory was dissolved in 1536 and the site was granted to Richard Codington. The prior, William Blome, was given a pension of £20; the remaining monks had to go to larger monasteries or leave penniless.

Leiston Abbey

Leiston Abbey (OS grid reference TM 4448 6416) was a Premonstratensian abbey dedicated to the Blessed Virgin; it was founded in 1182 by Ranulph de Glanville, Henry II's Lord Chief Justice, for 26 canons. The site is maintained by English Heritage and the ruins are open to the public.

Beginnings of the abbey

The original abbey was built about a mile and a half south-west of the site, in the marshes at Minsmere; however, the area was prone to severe flooding, so in 1365 the monks asked the pope for a licence to move inland. The new abbey was built by Robert de Ufford and it burned down in 1389, but was rebuilt.

Leiston Abbey. Photograph by author.

Scandals

The houses of the white canons were all exempt from the visitation of the bishop in their diocese, but commissaries from the abbey at Prémontré visited regularly. At

Remains of Leiston Abbey; plate from Thomas Kitson Cromwell's Excursions Through Suffolk, *1818-9. Photograph by author.*

the 1488 visitation, Robert Colvyll and three other canons were given a day's punishment for breaking silence, and the visitor complained about the monks' tonsures, but otherwise all was well.

In 1500, there were more problems; at the visitation, Thomas March or Marsch was accused of being an apostate (leaving the religious life for a secular one without permission) because he went outside the precincts without permission. He was originally sentenced to 20 days' penance, but everyone in the abbey asked for him to be let off and the bishop agreed to suspend the penalty. The bishop also said that each chamber of the dormitory should have a window, and the canons had to use simple cowls instead of ones with tails.

Dissolution and after

The abbey was suppressed in 1536; in 1537, the site was granted to Charles Brandon, Duke of Suffolk. George Carleton, the last abbot, was given a pension of £20.

The abbey became a farm and a farmhouse was built in the ruins. In 1928, Ellen Wrightson bought the abbey and used it as a religious retreat. She died in 1946 and left the abbey to the Diocese of St Edmundsbury and Ipswich, and in 1977 it was bought by the Pro Corda Trust, the National School for Young Chamber Music Players, a charity which runs chamber music courses for children.

In August 2004, during a dig organised by Suffolk County Council, a monk's skull and upper body was discovered by a teenager.

The legend of the holy thorn

At one point, there was meant to be a holy thorn in the abbey grounds that flowered on Christmas day. It was meant to be an offshoot of Joseph of Arimathea's staff; similar stories are told of the thorn at Parham in Suffolk and Hethel in Norfolk.

Secret tunnels and hidden treasure

At Dissolution, it's said that the commissioners could only find £40 of treasure, even though the abbey had an annual income of £181; legend says that the rest is buried somewhere in the cloisters.

There are also supposed to be secret tunnels running from the abbey. One is meant to run to Greyfriars Priory at Dunwich, and another to Framlingham Castle. The usual truth behind these legendary tunnels is that they're drainage channels. However, there's an interesting story about the tunnel leading to Framlingham; allegedly, a sow and her litter once went down the tunnel and they were never seen again. This is very similar to a tale told about one of the legendary tunnels beneath Norwich Castle.

Lidgate Castle

The remains of Lidgate Castle (OS grid reference TL 7212 5819) are the motte and bailey, which were built in the mid-twelfth century, and the 50-feet-deep ditches. They can still be seen from the edge of the churchyard wall, behind the church tower, but are on private land with no public right of access.

Looking down into the ditch of Lidgate Castle, viewed from behind the church tower. Photograph by author.

The beginning of the castle

The origins of the castle lie further back, however. It was originally an Iron Age hill fort, built to protect travellers on the Icknield Way, the 'Devil's ditch', and the community. Roman bricks have also been found in the churchyard of St Mary's – the present-day use of the Bailey – so it's possible that a Roman garrison was stationed there.

During the time of Edward the Confessor, Lidgate was administered by the Thane Stori, and the village was under the authority of the abbey of Bury St Edmunds.

William the Conqueror gave Lidgate to Reynold sans Nase for service at the Battle of Hastings; by 1086 it was owned by William de Waterville, and in 1110 by Reginald de Scanceler. When de Scanceler went on a crusade and didn't return, Lidgate reverted to the abbey of Bury St Edmunds.

The castle was probably built in 1043, but had gone by the time the church was built in 1250. According to Augustine Page, in his supplement to Kirby's *Suffolk Traveller*, the people of Lidgate called the area King John's Castle, and its ruins were used to repair roads in the neighbourhood.

During the civil war between Stephen and Matilda, the abbey took Matilda's side, and it's thought that Maurice de Windsor refortified the castle.

The first baron, Sir Henry Hastyngs, was Lord of the Manor. He joined Simon de Montfort's revolt against Henry III, and in 1264 at the Battle of Lewes his forces defeated the king. He was also the constable of Kenilworth castle and defended it against the king; he also captured Kirtling Castle from the de Tosney family and took hostages, as well as taking Ely and threatening Cambridge, and marched on Norwich, He died at the age of 36, shortly after being pardoned.

From then on, the lords of the manor tended to be absentee landlords, and the castle fell into decline.

John Lydgate

The monastic poet John Lydgate was born in the village in around 1371; he was educated at the monastery in Bury St Edmunds and was ordained as a priest in 1397. He was one of the best-known and most prolific writers in 15th-century England and spent eight years translating and expanding Guido delle Colonne's *Historia destructionis Troiae*, commissioned by the Black Prince (later Henry V), as well as writing a life of St Edmund. In his biographical *Testament*, Lydgate described himself as a mischievous boy who scrumped apples, hated getting up for matins, didn't wash before dinner, and who threw his choirbooks at a cockerel.

This particular poem also described whee he was born:

> Born in a village which is called Lydgate,
> By olde time a famous castle towne
> In Danes time it was beate down:
> Time what St Edmund martir maid and King was slain.

Lydgate continued to have Lancastrian patronage, and went into service with the Earl of Warwick in Paris. He was prior of Hatfield Regis in Essex from 1423 to 1434, although he spent most of his time in Bury, London and France. William Curteys, the abbot of Bury, asked Lydgate to write the legend of St Edmund for Henry VI; the poem spans three book and 3700 lines.

He died in about 1450 at Bury and was buried in the abbey chapel, with an epitaph which (according to Tanner's *Monastica*) described him as 'qui fuit quondam celebris Brittaniae fama Poesis' ('who was once renowned poet of famous Britain').

Lindsey Castle

L indsey Castle (OS grid reference TL 9799 4411) is the 12th-century remains of a motte with baileys dating to the later medieval period. The motte is 4 metres tall and the ditch is 3 metres deep; no flint wall or remains are visible, and the area is covered in trees and shrubs. The castle is on private land, but the chapel of St James – which belonged to the castle – is looked after by English Heritage and is accessible to the public.

The beginnings of the castle

The castle was an adulterine castle built during the reign of Stephen; it's possible that it was built by Adam de Cokefield, and there are monastic chronicles which states that Adam was able to defend the villages of Groton and Semer and 'had a castle of his own... namely the castle of Lelesey [Lindsey]'. The chronicle of Jocelin de Brakelond, a monk from Bury St Edmunds, also refers to a castle at Lindsey.

Adam died in the 1150s, and his grandson Robert – who was the custodian of the Abbot's estates in Bury St Edmunds – lived there in 1180. Although Henry II had demolished most of the adulterine castles, Lindsey appears to have been saved, possibly by intervention of the Abbot of Bury St Edmunds. Robert's son Adam inherited the castle, but died in 1198 and left the castle to his three-month-old daughter, Nesta de Cokefield.

On 27 May 1204 King John gave Thomas de Burgh permission to fortify 'Leleshay' (Lindsey). It's possible that Thomas was Nesta's guardian; we know that she was to marry John de Bello Campo, and they gave the church of Lindsey to Kersey Priory in 1240, but kept the rights to the chapel of St James. The castle was abandoned at some time before the end of the 13th century.

Lindsey chapel. Photograph by author.

The chapel of St James the Apostle

The chapel of St James probably existed in the 12th century but was rebuilt in the 13th century and was dedicated to James the Apostle. As well as being a domestic chapel to the castle, it was also a chantry and college. In 1242, Nesta de Cokefield imposed the 'Lindsey Tithe' on lands in Cockfield; the

The interior of Lindsey chapel. Photograph by author.

money was used to keep continual lighting in the chapel of St James. Eventually the manor and the chapel passed to the de Sampson family; there are records of them appointing wardens of the chapel in 1375, 1400 and 1408.

The college at Lindsey – along with all similar colleges – was dissolved in 1547; the land was given to Thomas Turner. Shortly afterwards, it was converted into a barn; the building was given to the nation in 1930 and is now in the care of English Heritage.

Little Wenham Hall

Little Wenham Hall. Photograph by author.

Little Wenham Hall; plate from Thomas Kitson Cromwell's Excursions Through Suffolk, 1818-9. Photograph by author.

Little Wenham Hall (OS grid reference TM 0807 3907) is moated, fortified manor house dating from the 13th century, and is one of the earliest brick buildings in the country. It is a private residence and there is no access to the public, but you can see the castle from St Lawrence's churchyard.

The house was built some time between 1260 and 1290 from flint, tile and Belgian brick. It was built by specialists from Belgium, as builders in England had not yet learned to work with brick; the base of the walls is more than a metre thick, and the ground floor of the house is rib-vaulted. There is a French inscription over the main entrance: *Cecy fait à l'aide de Dieu l'an de Grace 1569* (this was made with the help of God in the year of grace 1569). It's likely that the original main entrance was on the first floor in the west wall; however, the steps are missing.

The house is partially moated, and there are remains of a square bailey. As the Bigods managed the estate for the Bishop of Bayeux in the 11th century, it's possible that there was a 'proper' castle at Little Wenham in the Norman period.

We know that Little Wenham Hamm was originally owned by the Vaux family; in 1287 it was inherited by Petronilla de Nerford – and the chapel in the house is dedicated to St Petronilla.

By 1331, the house had passed to Gilbert de Debenham, who died in 1371. It remained in the de Gilbert family until the end of the 15th century, and survived an attack by Lancastrian sympathisers in 1470. Gilbert de Debenham V died in about 1500 (either in prison or on the scaffold) and his sister, Dame Elizabeth Brewes, inherited the house. The house was altered in about 1569, and again in the 19th and 20th centuries.

Lowestoft Witches' Stones

There is a tradition at Lowestoft that there was a monastery in the town, but there is no physical or documentary evidence to prove it; the so-called 'undercrofts' are really 14th-century merchants' cellars. Unsurprisingly, there are meant to be many secret tunnels leading from the undercrofts, and it's a fair bet that many of them were involved in smuggling.

The Witches' Stones and Belle Vue Park

Just within the southern entrance to Belle Vue Park you can see a heap of small of small stones, roughly cemented together; on top is a rusty anchor. They're known as the 'witches' stones'. Belle Vue Park was laid out in 1874, but there is photographic evidence showing that the stones were there in 1862 – and in fact the stones were there long before that, as they're the remains of a beacon tower that was set up on the cliffs in 1550 to act as a warning in case of invasion by the Spanish. A second tower was originally placed at the top of Links Road (Green Score) but there are no remains.

Legends of the Stones

Several legends have grown up about the stones. One says that if you pour water over them, rain will start to fall. Another says that if they're not bathed in fire, they rise up when the town hall clock starts to chime midnight, rush down to the sea for a dip (or a drink), and return to their place before the last stroke of midnight has chimed.

The witches' stones, Belle Vue Park, Lowestoft. Photograph by author.

How did they get the name? It isn't clear, but it's tempting to link them to the Lowestoft witches, Amy Denny (or Duny) and Rose Cullender – some sources say that Amy used to sit on the stones and shout abuse at people, although this wasn't mentioned in her trial.

The Lowestoft Witches

Samuel Pacy was a wealthy fish-merchant in Lowestoft; he'd refused to sell fish to Amy Denny, a poor widow, because she had the reputation of being a witch. After he'd refused to sell her some fish for the third time, his 9-year-old daughter Deborah 'was taken with most violent fits, feeling most extream pain in her Stomach, like the pricking of Pins, and Shreeking out in a most dreadful manner like unto a Whelp, and not like unto a sensible Creature'. This went on for three weeks, and Pacy asked his neighbour, Dr Feavor, to look at her. (The two doctors listed in the town at the time were James Reeve and Robert Peake – and there are no records of a 'Dr Feavor'.) Feavor couldn't find any natural causes for the child's illness; and when Deborah had her next fit, according to Pacy, she 'would cry out of *Amy Duny* as the cause of her Malady, and that she did affright her with Apparitions of her Person'.

Pacy made a formal complaint, and Amy was put in the stocks on 28 October. Two days later, Pacy's eldest daughter, 11-year-old Elizabeth, 'fell into extream fits, insomuch, that they could not open her Mouth to give her breath, to preserve her Life without the help of a Tap which they were enforced to use...'

Over the next two months, the sisters periodically lost their ability to see, speak or hear – sometimes for days – and complained of feeling sore or being lame. If they heard the words 'Lord', 'Jesus' or 'Christ', they had fits; and they claimed that Rose Cullender (another alleged witch) and Amy Denny appeared before them, shaking their fists and 'threatning, *That if they related either what they saw or heard, that they would Torment them Ten times more than ever they did before.*'

When they coughed or vomited, they brought up pins and 'a Two-penny Nail with a very broad head' – which their parents considered absolute proof that they were bewitched.

They went to stay with an aunt, Margaret Arnold, at the end of November 1661. Margaret believed they were faking the fits, and tried an experiment; she removed all the pins from their clothes. But then the girls started vomiting up pins, and claimed that bees and flies had forced pins into their mouths. And then one of the girls – though it isn't clear from the 1682 pamphlet giving details of the trial – said that Amy had been with her and '*that she tempted her to Drown her self; and to cut her Throat, or otherwise to Destroy her self.*'

The formal indictment took place at the Bury St Edmunds Assizes on 10 March 1662 in front of judge Sir Matthew Hale, the lord chief baron of the court of the exchequer and the leading legan scholar of the time. By then, three other girls had claimed to be bewitched by Amy and Rose: Ann Durrant, 14-year-old Jane Bocking and 18-year-old Susan Chandler. Deborah and Jane were too ill to attend the trial; but Elizabeth, Ann and Susan came to court. As soon as they walked in with their respective families, to present the bills of indictment, they had a fit; when they recovered, they were all unable to speak for the rest of the trial.

Firstly, Dorothy Durrant (no relation to Ann) accused Amy of bewitching and murdering her 10-year-old daughter, four years before – why she waited so long to accuse Amy was never explained. Dorothy's story was that Amy had bewitched her son William while child-minding him. Dr Jacobs from Yarmouth had told her to hang William's blanket over the fireplace and burn anything that fell from it. A large toad duly fell out of the blanket; when it was held in tongs over the fire, it exploded with a flash of light and no remains could be found. The next day, one of Amy's relatives told Dorothy that Amy had burns all over her body (even though later there were no scars to be seen). Amy allegedly cursed Dorothy, saying that she would outlive some of her children and be forced to live on crutches. (Given child mortality rates of the time, this was hardly the 'curse' it was claimed to be – most parents outlived at least one of their children.) Elizabeth then fell ill and died, after claiming that she'd seen Amy's ghost; and Dorothy became lame and was forced to use crutches. The judge suggested that there might be natural causes for Dorothy's lameness, but she was adamant that it was due to witchcraft.

Next, Elizabeth Pacy came into court – struck dumb, lying on cushions on her back, and the only signs of life being her breathing. The judge brought Amy in to the court, and Amy touched the child's hand; instantly, Elizabeth leapt up, eyes closed, and grabbed Amy's hand and then her face, scratching her hard enough to draw blood and not stopping until Amy was forcibly taken away.

The parents of Ann, Jane and Susan made their statements next, saying that their children had been affected in the same way as the Pacy girls – stomach pains, vomiting up pins (which were produced in court – as were more than 40 pins and the nail that the Pacy girls had vomited up), fits, and claiming that they'd seen the ghosts of Amy or Rose. Ann Durrant was brought into court, and as soon as she was brought near Rose she started having fits.

The court asked Sir Thomas Browne, the Norwich doctor and author of *Religio Medici*, to give evidence. He said he believed that witches existed, and in his view the children had been bewitched, and that the women had used 'the same method of afflicting persons' as witches in Denmark.

The court then carried out tests. In the first one, while the girls were having fits and their fists were tightly closed, 'as yet the strongest Man in the Court could not force them open' – but when Rose Cullender touched them lightly, the girls shrieked and their fists opened.

Next, the court blindfolded Elizabeth and got her to touch Amy and another woman – the idea being that if Elizabeth touched the witch she would scream, and if she touched an innocent woman she'd be silent. However, Elizabeth reacted the same way to both women, shrieking her head off. The judges – Lord Charles Cornwallis, a county magistrate; Sir Edmund Bacon, the county JP; and Sir John Keeling, later chief justice of the King's Bench – came straight back into court, saying that 'they did believe the whole transaction of this business was a meer Imposture'. Samuel Pacy refuted this, saying that it proved the allegation because the power of the witch was so strong that it made her believe she was touching a witch when she wasn't – in his words, she'd been 'deceived by a suspicion that the Witch touched her when she did not'.

More complaints followed. John Soan said that Rose had bewitched one of his three carts and made it unusable for a day; it had crashed into her house and damaged a window, and she'd shouted at him. That day, the cart that had damaged her house overturned several times, stuck in a gateway and the men couldn't unload it – though there were no problems with the other two carts.

Robert Sherringham said that one of his carts had damaged her house two years before and she'd said his horses would suffer for it; four of his horses died shortly afterwards, and all his piglets died shortly after birth; he also claimed that she'd caused him to be lame and suffer from a 'number of Lice of extraordinary bigness'. The only way he could get rid of the lice was to burn both his suits. (Interestingly, Rose was found 'not guilty' of this indictment.)

Ann Sandeswell – the wife of Amy's landlord – complained of the loss of geese and fish, eight years before.

Rose and Amy pleaded not guilty; but the jury had been impressed by Elizabeth scratching Rose's face. Half an hour later, they returned their verdict: guilty. The following day, Pacy claimed that all the children were 'cured' within a few minutes of the conviction, and Dorothy Durrant was able to throw her crutches away and walk normally again.

Rose and Amy were hanged on 17 March 1662, still protesting their innocence.

The Ghost of Edward Rollahide

According to Lowestoft historian Jack Rose, the ghost of Edward Rollahide haunts the North Quay at Lowestoft. So the story goes, Rollahide was working on the construction of the quay in 1921; he was playing cards with a colleague, George Turner, when a row broke out. Rollahide picked up an axe and started to chase Turner – but then he lost his balance and fell into a pit of cement; he was never seen alive again and was thought to have drowned. Turner came home from work one evening, after a visit to the pub, and was terrified when Rollahide's ghost appeared before him, dripping cement and swinging an axe before disappearing through a wall. Turner died a few days later from the shock, and it's said that Rollahide's ghost has been seen at least three times since.

Martello Towers

Martello tower at Aldeburgh Photograph by author.

Martello towers were built along the south and east coast between Aldeburgh and Sussex between 1803 and 1812 to resist any attempted invasion by Napoleon.

The idea came during the war in Corsica, when the Royal Navy went to the aid of Corsican patriots against the French and bombarded the large round tower on Mortella Point. They'd already captured the tower in September 1793, when *HMS Lowestoft* bombarded it for two hours, but the Corsican patriots lost it to the French again. In February 1794, *HMS Fortitude* and *HMS Juno* sailed into Fiorenzo bay and attacked the tower; although they were repulsed, the British Army had landed further up the coast, besieged the tower and took it.

Vice-Admiral Hood later reported of the battle at sea:

> The *Fortitude* and *Juno* were ordered against it, without making the least impression by a continued cannonade of two hours and a half; and the

former ship being very much damaged by red-hot shot, both hauled off. The walls of the Tower were of a prodigious thickness, and the parapet, where there were two eighteen-pounders, was lined with bass junk, five feet from the walls, and filled up with sand; and although it was cannonaded from the Height for two days, within 150 yards, and appeared in a very shattered state, the enemy still held out; but a few hot shot setting fire to the bass, made them call for quarter. The number of men in the Tower were 33; only two were wounded, and those mortally.

The tower at Mortella was demolished before the British left in 1796, but the tower's defensive strength impressed Admiral Sir John Jervis, the Commander-in-Chief of the Mediterranean, who wrote that he 'hoped to see such works erected on every part of the [English] coast likely for an enemy to make a descent on.'

Thus the idea of Martello towers was born; the word was a corruption of 'Mortella', although there is also some confusion with the 'torre de martello' or hammer towers used on the Italian coast, where a hammer struck a bell to warn that pirates were approaching.

The East coast towers were built to stop Napoleon's armies marching on London from the east; because the east coast isn't quite as steep as the south coast, the Martello towers there are larger than those built on the south coast. They were mini forts, built from stone or rendered brick. The ground floor acted as the magazine and store room; the garrison (usually one officer and 24 men) lived on the first floor in a 'casemate', which was divided into several rooms and had fireplaces for cooking and heating; and on the roof cannon were mounted on pivots so they could be turned through 360 degrees. There was usually a well or cistern for fresh water, and some had a drainage system to refill the cistern with rainwater.

Around 29 towers were built between Aldeburgh (OS grid reference TM 46296 54908) and St Osyth in Essex; 18 of them survive (12 of them in Suffolk), and three of them are on the Buildings at Risk Register. The towers were thicker at the front than at the back, and it's said that each tower took 700,000 bricks to build.

They were never actually used during the Napoleonic Wars; after the threat from the French receded, some were demolished or swept away by coastal erosion, others were made into homes, and some were taken over by the coastguard and used to fight against smuggling. During the Second World War, some Martello towers acted as observation platforms.

The Towers of Suffolk

The towers were all designated with letters of the alphabet. Tower L, at Shotley Gate, is on a site that may be developed as retirement housing. Tower M, on the River Orwell near Shotley Marina, was once used as a water tower but is currently unused. Tower N was located at Walton Ferry in Felixstowe and the site is under the docks. Tower O, on the tip of Langer Point, was destroyed by coastal erosion. Tower P is on Felixstowe seafront; the moat was filled in, and it has been used by the coastguard. Tower Q is also at Felixstowe, at Bulls Cliff, and was converted into a house in 1946.

Tower R was thought to be lost, but when Bartlett Hospital applied to be a listed building, it was discovered that the tower is part of the hospital foundations; Tower S was nearby and was abandoned in 1835. Tower T is within Felixstowe golf club. Tower U, on the River Deben, is now a private house; facing it, on the opposite side of the river, was Tower V, which was destroyed in 1819. Tower W, at Bawdsey Cliffs, was converted to a house in the 1980s; it was at risk from erosion, but sea defences have been built to protect it. Tower X was further along the beach, and was dismantled after 1870; the foundations were used as part of a World War II gun emplacement. Tower Y, also in Bawdsey, was converted to a house. Tower Z, at Alderton, is on the 'at risk' register. Tower AA, near Hollesley, was converted into a house; Tower BB, on a shingle bank near the mouth of the River Ore, was pulled down in 1822. Tower CC, ten miles down the coast at Aldeburgh (Slaughden), is the largest; its design is unusual, with four concentric brick bastions surrounded by a dry moat. Originally, it had four 24-pounder guns on the roof. As at 2007, around a third of the moat has been lost to coastal erosion. The tower itself has been restored and is used as a holiday cottage. And although there aren't any actual ghost stories associated with the towers, holidaymakers have described the cellars as 'spooky'...

Mettingham Castle

Mettingham Castle gateway.
Photograph by author.

Mettingham Castle curtain wall.
Photograph by author.

Mettingham Castle (OS grid reference TM 360 887) is the earthworks, gateway and ruins of a 14th-century fortified manor house and a later college; the site covers about five acres. It's on private land and there are occasional open days for visitors, though some of the ruins can be seen from the road.

The beginnings of the castle

The castle was built by Sir John de Norwich; there is a licence dated 21 August 1343, giving him permission from Edward III to crenellate his manor house in return for his services during the French wars. In the summer of 1340, there were reports that a huge French armada was gathering at Sluys, on the Belgian coast, intending to destroy the English shipping and then attack England. Edward III gathered his fleet; it's possibly that Sir John de Norwich commanded the flcet in the Orwell estuary.

When the 400 French ships met the 300 English ships in the Zwin channel, the English had the advantage of the wind and tide behind them, and 500 archers fought valiantly from 8am to 7pm. Only 30 French boats escaped, and the English won the day.

Sir John died in 1361 and his tomb is in the church at Mettingham. Some sources say that his grandson, also Sir John, inherited the castle; when he did in 1373. The house and land went to his cousin, Katherine de Brewes, who was a nun in Kent. She gave the castle to a secular college – i.e. clergy who didn't take monastic vows – and, after a row with the nuns at Bungay, the college finally moved there in 1393 with a master and 13 chaplains. The college occupied the mansion, and built a new chapel between 1414 and 1424; they also added two 'lavatoria' to the cloisters in 1424.

Remains of Mettingham Castle; plate from Thomas Kitson Cromwell's Excursions Through Suffolk, *1818-9. Photograph by author.*

The end of the castle

The college was dissolved in 1535 and the site was granted to Sir Anthony Denny. A document of 1562 says that the site was enclosed by a stone wall and entered via a gatehouse. Inside were stables, servants' lodgings, a kitchen, a bakehouse, a brewhouse, a malting house, storehouses and an aisled hall.

In 1565, the building was described as 'utterly decayed'. Most of it was demolished in the 18th century, and the last corner tower (known as Kate's Tower, after Katherine de Brews, according to a report in the *Ipswich Journal* in 1861) fell in 1830. Mr Safford, the owner, replaced the building by a house; in turn, the house was demolished in about 1880.

The Castle in the Rising of 1381

The castle was attacked by a mob led by Walter Coselere on 18 June 1381. The mob seized goods and arms worth £1,000, plus £40 in cash; they also took away the court rolls, extents and surveys. The following day, John Wrawe (the parson of Ringsfield Church, who led most of the Suffolk rebellion) attacked the unoccupied castle with a mob of 500 men; they took £40 in gold and silver and £20 of goods, before heading off to Beccles.

Orford Castle

| Orford Castle. Photograph by author. | View from the top of Orford Castle. Photograph by author. |

O rford Castle (OS grid reference TM 41942 49873) is the remains of a 12th-century castle on Castle Green, at the western edge of the village of Orford; although Augustine Page, in his supplement to Kirby's *Suffolk Traveller* in the mid-19th century, says that 'the spot whereon the castle stands was, it is said, formerly the centre of the town.'

The keep – which is 30 metres high and built from four different types of stone – is in the care of English Heritage, and is open to the public.

The beginnings of the castle

Henry II built the castle as a sea defence, and also as a way of upholding his authority in a region where there were many castles belonging to Hugh Bigod, the Earl of Norfolk, who was a known rebel (see Bungay Castle, page 12). It's the earliest castle in England that still has documentary evidence of the construction; the Pipe Rolls say that it was built between 1165 and 1173 at a total cost of £1414, 9s and 2d (nearly a tenth of the king's annual income). We know that two-thirds of the money was spent in the first two years of building, and that the first constable, appointed in 1167, was Bartholomew de Granville, who was paid £20 a year.

The keep is of a really unusual polygonal design, with 18 sides and three projecting towers; this means that there are no blind spots and all sides of the castle could be defended easily. There are four different types of stone within the keep: a

Remains of Orford Castle, showing the now-lost curtain wall; plate from Thomas Kitson Cromwell's Excursions Through Suffolk, *1818-9. Photograph by author.*

local mudstone called septaria was used externally, along with limestone from Northamptonshire, and internally local corraline crag was used with Caen stone from Normandy for the fine details. The walls are 20 feet thick at the base.

It was also one of the earliest castles in the country to use mural or flanking towers along the curtain wall, although the keep is the only surviving structure of the castle nowadays; the last bit of the curtain walls fell in 1840. If any invaders managed to get past the curtain walls, they'd have to negotiate the steps to the keep, where they would be picked off by archers. However, is worth noting that the holes in the turret are not actually murder holes; they're vents for the kitchen fires. The archers would have worked from platforms on top of the turrets; there were crenels (a form of shutters) between the battlements, which were hinged so the archers could shoot out, then let the flap fall back to protect them.

The Siege of 1173

In 1173, Hugh Bigod joined Henry II's sons, Henry and Robert, the Earl of Leicester, in a rebellion against the king. Their army of Flemish mercenaries had been repulsed at Dunwich (see page 51), but landed at Walton and failed to capture the castle there (see page 67). They marched to Orford, hoping to attack the king's new stronghold; but the castle had been garrisoned with extra troops (70 men, and Ralph le Breton was paid compensation 'for his houses which were carried into the castle'), and the castle records show that the castle was well provisioned with bacon, cheese, salt, iron, tallow, ropes and mills for grinding corn.

Although the Flemish mercenaries captured the coal from the castle, the castle repulsed the invaders and the rebels went to regroup at Framlingham. When Hugh and the rebels were overcome in 1174, the fine that Hugh had to pay went a good way to reimbursing the cost of building Orford. The castle was then reinforced.

Capture by the French, 1217

In 1217, the year after the death of King John, the rebel barons supported the claim of Louis, Dauphin of France, to the English throne. Louis – later Louis IX – captured Orford. However, when he was defeated in May 1217 at the Battle of Lincoln, the castle returned to the English royal forces, and was repaired.

Scandals – Hugh of Dennington

Hugh of Dennington was the constable of the castle in the 1270s. However, he wasn't known for treating men kindly – he imprisoned one royal official for three days, and another prisoner died from his injuries and his corpse was thrown out to sea.

The End of the Castle

From around 1280, the Crown lost interest in Orford – partly because the harbour was silting up and business was being transferred to other ports. The castle was rented out to Robert of Ufford in 1280, then Roger Bigod in 1302 and Robert of Ufford (the younger) in 1330. In 1336, Edward III sold it to Robert and made him the Earl of Suffolk.

Although there were a couple of times during this period when the castle was garrisoned – in 1297 when a rebellion was threatened against Edward I, and again in 1307 when rebellion was threatened against Edward II. There are records of ten men 'guarding the castle with cross-bows, bows, arrows and other arms' in 1301, when they were paid 3d a day.

Gradually the castle fell into decline, although the prison was sometimes used to hold criminals from Orford. It was bought by the Stanhope family in the 1590s; he took much of the stone from the castle site to build the foundations of his new home at Sudbourne Hall. The castle continued to decline, and in 1753 it was sold to the Earl of Hertford. The second Marquis, in 1805, planned to demolish the castle and reuse the materials; however, as the castle was used as a seamark to help shipping avoid a dangerous sandbank, the government persuaded him to change his mind. During the Napoleonic wars, the castle – despite being in a ruinous state – came back into use, as a signalling mast was put up on the south turret.

The third Marquis of Hertford had more of an antiquarian's instinct and wanted to preserve the ruins; in 1831 he gave the castle a new floor and a conical roof. The keep was used for banquets and private parties, and the grounds were used for picnics. When the fourth Marquis died in 1870, his son Sir Richard Wallace inherited much of his money. The following year, he bought the castle from the fifth Marquis, and although he sold it on in 1885 he kept several items relating to Orford and they became part of the Wallace Collection.

In 1928 Sir Arthur Churchman bought the castle and presented it to the Orford Town Trust; two years later, it was opened to the public.

In 1962 the castle was put in the care of the state, and remains open to the public.

The Castle in the Second World War

During the Second World War, the castle was requisitioned and a reinforced concrete roof was built at the top of the south eastern turret. Originally, the roof was meant to hold an anti-aircraft gun, but was actually used as a radar observation post.

The Orford Merman

There is a very strange story about the Merman of Orford, which was first written down by Ralph de Coggeshall in 1207. He says that the events took place during the reign of Henry I, when Bartholomew de Glanville was the constable; the historian Stowe places the year as in 1167.

So the story goes, some fishermen in Orford caught a monster in their nets. They said he looked like a man in the shape and size; he was naked, covered with hair – except on his head, which was bald – and had a long shaggy beard. The fishermen took him to the constable of the castle, who kept him for several times.

Allegedly, the wild man would eat whatever food he was given, but would squash it between his hands until all the juice had been squeezed out; he particularly liked to eat fish. However, he refused to talk, even when the men in the castle tortured him and hung him up by his feet. He used to go to bed at sunset, and get up at sunrise. Although they took him into church, Ralph said that the merman 'showed no signs of reverence or belief'.

One day, the guards took the merman out to sea; they spread three rows of strong nets to stop him escaping but, the water clearly being his element, he dived straight under the nets and appeared on the other side of the barriers. The guards, fairly chastened by the fact that they had let the merman go so easily, went back to the castle; however, they were surprised to discover that the merman followed them. He continued living with them for a while, but eventually grew weary of living ashore and left again, never to be seen again.

He was probably kept in the castle prison, which is sited beneath a trapdoor in the lobby and is not accessible to visitors.

The Dragon from the Sea

In 1749, the *Gentleman's Magazine* carried a story about the sea-dragon of Orford, which allegedly attacked several fishermen after they snared it in their nets off the coast of Orford. After they killed it, they took it round the country as a curiosity; sadly, what happened to the body is unknown, and there appear to be no engravings of the creature. However, we do have an account of what it looked like, from the writer of the *Gentleman's Magazine*:

> Its head and tail resemble those of an alligator; it has two large fins, which serve it both to swim and to fly; and though they were so dried that I could not extend them, yet they appear, by the folds, to be shaped like those which painters have given to dragons and other winged monsters that serve as supporters to coats of arms. Its body is covered with impenetrable scales; its legs have two joints, and its feet are hoofed like those of an ass: it has five rows of very white and sharp teeth in each jaw, and is in length about 4 feet, though it was longer when alive it having shrunk as it became dry.
>
> It was caught in a net with mackerel; and being dragged on shore, was knocked down with a stretcher or boat-hook. The net being opened, it suddenly sprung up, and flew above 50 yards: the man who first seized it had several of his fingers bitten off; and the wound mortifying, he died. It afterwards fastened on the man's arm who shows it, and lacerated it so much, that the muscles are shrunk, and the hand and fingers distorted; the wound is not yet healed, and is thought to be incurable. It is said by some to have been described by naturalists under the name of the *Sea-dragon*.

The *Encyclopaedia Britannica* of 1810, although repeating the story, loftily added that 'we think it extremely probable that the animal was nothing more than a distorted or overgrown individual of some of the well known species of fish'. The description of the teeth and the skin do sound quite like those of a shark, and it's possible that the 'wings' were fins; however, the legs and cloven feet are not particularly shark-like. So what the fishermen actually caught is very much open to speculation…

Redlingfield Nunnery

Old sign of Redlingfield in porch of church, showing priory church. Photograph by author.

Redlingfield village sign, showing priory church and guest house. Photograph by author.

Redlingfield Nunnery (OS grid reference TM 1863 7067) is the ruins of a Benedictine Nunnery; the surviving remains are the chapel, now used as the parish church, and part of the guest house, now used as a barn. The barn is on private lands, although it can be seen from the churchyard.

The Beginnings of the Nunnery

The nunnery was founded in 1120 by Manasses, Earl of Guisnes, and Emma, his wife, who was also the daughter of the Lord of Redlingfield. It was dedicated to St Andrew. In 1291, it was exempt from the taxation roll, probably owing to poverty,

Scandals – the banishment of Isabel Hermyte

On 9 September 1427, William Alnwick, the bishop of Norwich, sent Thomas Ryngstede, the dean of the college of St Mary in the Fields, to do the visitation of Redlingfield Nunnery; it's the only visitation of a monastic community recorded in Alnwick's book. Unusually, the nuns were examined in both Latin and English.

Redlingfield church, formerly used as the chapel for the priory. Photograph by author.

Ryngstede assembled the nuns in the chapter house: Isabel Hermyte, the prioress; Alice Lampit, the sub-prioress; five nuns and two novices.

And then he heard Isabel's confession. She said that on 25 January 1425 she'd promised on oath to observe the biship's injunctions – but since then she'd never been to confession, and she hadn't observed Sundays or principal feasts. She also admitted that she and one of her novices, Joan Tates, had slept in a private chamber instead of in the dormitory with the other nuns; that she only had nine nuns instead of thirteen in the community; and there was only one chaplain instead of three.

Financially, too, she was in trouble; as with many priors, she hadn't done her annual accounts. She also admitted to taking goods, and

Barn at Redlingfield Hall, thought to have been formerly the priory guest house. Photograph by author.

having trees cut down and selling them without telling the rest of the convent or getting their consent.

Personally, she was accused of 'laying violent hands on Agnes Brakle on St Luke's Day' – but, far worse, she was 'de incontinentia scandalizata' with Thomas Langelond, the bailiff (in other words, she'd slept with him). She'd been alone with him in 'private and suspicious places', including a small hall with all the windows closed and 'sub heggerow' (i.e. underneath the hedgerow!).

Joan Tates, the novice, was also accused of incontinence (i.e. not keeping to her vow of chastity), and claimed that she'd been led into bad ways by the example of the prioress.

Two days later, to avoid a huge scandal, Isabel resigned; the document was witnessed by all the nuns.

Ryngstede's judgement was that they were all as bad as each other. He ordered that the whole convent should fast on Fridays, only having bread and beer. Joan Tates had admitted to incontinence, so she had go to in front of the convent the following Sunday, dressed in white flannel and wearing no veil. Isabel's confession was written in the diocesan register, and she was banished to the priory of Wykes.

Harsh Discipline

The next recorded visitation is on 7 August 1514, when Bishop Nix visited personally. The prioress complained that the nuns were disobedient, but the nuns complained that the sub-prioress was cruel and too harsh – she beat them the point where she drew blood.

As often in the priories, the prioress didn't produce accounts; but there were other problems. The nuns complained that boys (boarding scholars who were taught with their sisters) slept in the dormitory, and there weren't any curtains between the beds; also, there wasn't a proper infirmary and the refectory was used for other purposes instead of meals. The bishop clearly listened, because his injunctions said that the prioress had to give an inventory of valuable, movables and cattle before the feast of All Saints (1 November) and accounts by Michaelmas (29 September) the following year. The refectory and infirmary had to be used properly, and a warden appointed to the infirmary. The sub-prioress was told that she should correct and punish 'with discretion' – and the bishop added 'not cruelly'. Finally, they had to put curtains between the beds and boys weren't allowed to sleep in the dormitory.

The End of the Nunnery

The visitations of 1520, 1526 and 1532 were all fine. The nunnery was dissolved on 10 February 1536/7 and the house and site were granted to Sir Edmund Bedingfield. The nuns were all given 23s 4d and Grace Sampson, the prioress, was given a pension of 20 marks per year.

Rumburgh Priory

Rumburgh priory church. Photograph by author.

Rumburgh Priory (OS grid reference TM 3465 8187) is the remains of the Benedictine priory of St Michael and St Felix, and is one of the two pre-Conquest monastic houses in Suffolk (the other is Bury St Edmunds). The moat and the nave of the church (which also contains the priory arms) are the only visible remains; some stone has been reused in next-door Abbey Farm.

Rumburgh priory arms, on the wall of the church. Photograph by author.

The Beginnings of the Priory

The priory was founded between 1047 and 1067, by Aethelmar, the bishop of Elmham, and Abbot Thurston of St Benet of Hulme. Brother Blaker from Hulme was the prior, and there were 12 monks. According to the Domesday Book, the church at Rumburgh owned 40 acres, 6 borders, 1 plough team and wood for 6 hogs, together with rents from a hunting forest. Within 50 years, the priory had become a cell of St Mary's in York.

By 1258 there were only four monks, and by 1286 the numbers had dwindled to two.

Runaways

John de Guiseborough, of St Mary's in York, apparently ran away from the cell at Rumburgh in 1311, but returned two years later.

St Bee

Perhaps because of the Yorkshire connection, there was apparently a cult of St Bee at the priory; in the church, there was an image of the saint, and offerings of cheese and money were made to the image at Michaelmas.

Moat of Rumburgh priory. Photograph by author.

The end of the priory

The priory was suppressed in 1528 and the lands were given to Cardinal Wolsey for his college at Ipswich (see page 101).

The Abbot of St Mary's begged for the priory to remain part of his abbey, as it had for 300 years, rather than being suppressed. He wrote a letter to Wolsey explaining how little the priory was worth: 'for of trueth the rentes and revenuez unto the same priory belonging doith very lytill surmounte the sum of xxx.li sterling [£30], as far as I perceive.' He then offered Wolsey a compromise, if he'd leave the priory alone: 'And yet towardes your speciall, honourable and laudable purpose concernynge the erection and foundacion of the said college and scole, I am right interely contented, for your tenderinge of the premisses, to give unto your grace ccc. markes sterling, which shall be delivered to your grace immediately.'

Three hundred marks was equivalent to £200 – nearly seven times the value of the priory. So why would the abbot offer so much? Some sources say that the abbot had sent various items to Rumburgh for safekeeping – clearly worth more than the £200 he'd offered! – but Wolsey wasn't swayed.

After Wolsey's downfall, the site reverted to the Crown.

At dissolution, the monastery was 12,500 square feet, building around a rectangular cloister. The buttery was on the east, with possibly the sacristy and chapter house; on the west there was the prior's hall, guest bedrooms, and the kitchen. The refectory was on the north, with the parlour and solar; and the existing church and chancel was on the south. There were also lands of just over 267 acres, and outbuildings.

Sibton Abbey

Remains of Sibton Abbey; plate from Thomas Kitson Cromwell's Excursions Through Suffolk, *1818-9. Photograph by author.*

Sibton Abbey (OS grid reference TM 3650 6980) is the remains of a Cistercian monastery; it's the only Cistercian monastery in East Anglia, though there was a Cistercian nunnery at Marham in Norfolk. Although a 42-metre length of wall belonging to the south aisle of the church is still standing, it's on private land and isn't accessible to the public. You can see it from the road, but from a fairly dangerous corner, so it's only a fleeting view!

Beginnings of the Abbey

The abbey was founded in 1150 by William de Cheyney, the youngest son of Robert Fitzwalter, and dedicated to St Mary.

The Bishop of Norwich didn't visit the Cistercian houses, but in 1362 the Abbot of Warden did the abbey's visitation, and the records from the abbey actually detail his expenses. The total cost was £4 7s. 3d (the equivalent of about £1,450 in modern terms). They had to pay 13s. 8¾d for bread, beer, wine, fish, and horse-meat for the abbot and his train (which included two monks, two squires and three servants) to Bury St Edmunds. From Bury to Eye, the cost was 23¼d.; from Eye to Woodbridge,

Monks on Sibton village sign.
Photograph by author.

and returning to Ipswich, the cost was 20d.; and for spending a night at Ipswich and returning, 12s. 6½d. The remainder of the money was spent on entertaining the abbot and his train at the abbey.

In 1381 there were 11 monks at Sibton, though this had declined to 8 by 1536.

Dissolution

In 1536, the abbot sold the site and estates, worth £250, to the Duke of Norfolk; it was confirmed by Henry VIII, and the duke granted the abbey to Thomas Godsalve. Stone coffins were found here in 1832.

A Crime of Passion

In the cartulary of Sibton Abbey, document #817 tells the story of a crime of passion. Ailwy, a local man who changed his name to the more Norman-sounding Geoffrey, had two sons. The younger – Robert Malet – entered into the service of Hugh Bigod. The elder went on to have a son, whose temper got him into a huge mess. At one point, he found a man kissing his mistress – and was so angry that he killed the man. He was going to be executed for murder, but Robert Malet asked Hugh to intervene and obtain a pardon for his nephew from Henry II. Luckily for the boy, Robert had good connections with the court, and Hugh managed to obtain the pardon.

Southwold

The Ghosts of Gun Hill

Gun Hill takes its named from the cannon placed on them to overlook the sea, but surprisingly are not from the Battle of Sole Bay, fought off the coast of Southwold in 1672. The cannon are marked with the Tudor rose and crown, and are thought to be among the earliest cannon made in England. Tradition says that they were taken from Bonnie Prince Charlie at Culloden in 1746 by Duke of Cumberland (though it isn't known where they came from originally, or where Bonnie Prince Charlie captured them); however, as there is no proof that the Duke of Cumberland ever visited Southwold after Culloden, it's more likely that they were sent to Southwold during the Napoleonic wars to protect the coast. The guns needed 14 horses to pull each one.

One of the saddest ghosts to haunt Gun Hill is that of James Martin. The story is reported in the *Ipswich Journal,* following an inquest into the death of James Martin of the Coast Guard on. The inquest was held on Friday 11 November 1842 before the coroner, Charles Gross, and a jury:

> Whilst in the act of ramming the northernmost gun on the battery in Gun-hill, on the occasion of a salute fired on the anniversary of the birth-day of the Prince of Wales, was killed on the spot by the explosion of the charge. Verdict, 'Accidental Death.' The deceased was in his 30th year, and was much beloved by his comrades. He has left a widow and three young children.

James was looking after gun number one, and was reloading it for the second round when there was a misfire. He looked down the muzzle, and the delayed explosion blew his head off.

Cannons on Gun Hill, Southwold.
Photograph by author.

It's said that every so often, he returns to stand by the guns and faces the sea.

Because the Germans considered Southwold a fortified place and bombarded it in the First World War, the decision was taken to bury the cannons, so it's not sure which was Gun Number One.

Another ghost on the hill has been credited with a rescue. Two men saw a beautiful woman pass by and disappear behind the Round House. She was wearing a shawl over her head, and radiated a sense of peace. Wondering who she was, they followed her to the harbour; there was no trace of the woman, but they saw a capsized boat in the harbour and managed to rescue the sailor.

The Ghost of Southwold Beach
A ghostly fisherman has been seen walking on the beach, swinging a Tilly lamp and carrying a large fish.

The Earl of Sandwich and the Serving Girl
There's said to be a red-haired serving girl who haunts Sutherland House. During the Anglo-Dutch wars, the Duke of York had his headquarters at Sutherland

The beach at Southwold. Photograph by author.

House. The night before the Battle of Sole Bay in May 1672, the Earl of Sandwich stayed there overnight; he fell in love with one of the serving girls and spent the night making love with her. The next morning, he was late for battle – the last ship to join the fight – and was in such a hurry that he didn't say goodbye to her.

He died in the battle, and his body was washed ashore; he was only recognised because he was wearing the Order of the Garter. The broken-hearted serving girl is said to await his return, and it's said that sometimes you can smell fresh-baked bread at Sutherland House before the chefs have started for the day.

A wreck discovered offshore in the mid-1990s by local marine archaeologist Stuart Bacon is thought to be the *Royal James*, a ship of 1426 tons, which was built just before the battle; fishermen have bought up cannons balls in their nets, and two cannons have been raised.

The Fairy Hills
Thomas Kitson Cromwell, in his *Excursions Round Suffolk* (1819), says that on Eye Cliff and the surrounding area there are 'the vestiges of an ancient encampment, and where the ground has not been broken up, there are marks of circular tents, commonly called Fairy Hills'. Allegedly fairies used to dance round the circular marks. There were barrows in the area, but most of that section of cliffs has been eroded by the sea; Gun Hill (see above) is the only part that remains.

Sudbury Priory

The priory of Sudbury (OS grid reference TL 8707 4100) was a Dominican friary; it was established by Baldwin de Shipling and Chabil (or Mabel) his wife at some time before 1247, when Henry III gave the priory six marks towards its support.

Fights between town and gown

In August 1380, a row blew up after Simon, the Archbishop of Canterbury, and his brother John got permission to give the friars a piece of land in 'Babyngdonhall' (Ballingdon Hall) that contained a spring, and to make an aqueduct from the spring to their house. Local landowners protested so much that the work was delayed for five years – and the friars had to ask the king for royal protection for themselves, their servants, and the men they'd employed to make the aqueduct. The king also told the sheriff, mayor and bailiff of the town to defend the friars and stop any violence.

The end of the priory

The priory surrendered in 1539 and the land was granted to Thomas Eden, clerk of the king's council, and his wife Griselda. The priory was eventually demolished (in 1779, according to Kitson) and another house built on the suite.

Remains of the gateway to the priory at Friars Street, Sudbury. Photograph by author.

The site was excavated in 1970; archaeologists found remains of buildings, and also pottery dating from the 12th century date.

On the south side of Friar Street, there is a 'priory wall' – this isn't the actual priory, however, but from the 16th century gatehouse that was built shortly before Dissolution.

Scandals – John Hodgkin

John Hodgkin was one of the most prominent friars. He taught theology there, and in 1527 he was appointed to the office of Provincial of the English Dominicans. In

February 1529/30, the prior, Godfrey Jullys, gave him a house, garden and stabling at a very low rent, for as long as he was the Provincial. But in 1534 the royal court decided that Hodgkin wouldn't be on the right side – so they made sure that John Hilsey was appointed in his place.

Hodgkin wrote a letter to Cromwell, saying that he was 'ever ready to do in the most lowly manner such service as [he] shall be commanded' – and he was restored in 1536. The priory of Sudbury reduced his rent, hoping that he'd help them – but in 1537 he was appointed as the Bishop of Bedford, very much part of the new Protestant regime. He got married during the reign of Edward VI, but when Mary came to the throne he was thrown out. Hodgkin immediately repudiated his wife and explained that he was very penitent... and went back to being a Roman Catholic, getting a dispensation from Cardinal Pole. When Elizabeth came to the throne, he switched sides again – and took part in the ordination of several bishops.

Simon of Sudbury's skull and the haunted church

Simon of Sudbury, the Archbishop of Canterbury, was credited with inventing the poll tax – he'd accepted the post as the chancellor, and realised that the state coffers were empty. The crown jewels had been pawned to the City of London, the king was three months behind with his army's salary, and wool exports were down. Withdrawing from the war wasn't an option, so they were left with taxation. And that meant taxing everyone.

By the summer of 1381, the country had had enough. The causes of the revolt itself are complex – see Felixstowe Priory (page 69) for more details. Led by Wat Tyler, the rebels burned tax records and marched to London to demand fair treatment from the king – in particular, fair wages, the end of market monopolies and an end to the feudal system.

In London, Richard II met Tyler and the rebels at Mile End; he agreed to end serfdom and service to a feudal lord, to abolish market monopolies and abolish trade restrictions. Pleased with the result, Wat Tyler and the rebels next marched on the Tower of London, intent on getting rid of the man who'd thought up the tax. The Tower Guards gave them no resistance; Tyler's men found Simon of Sudbury praying in St John's chapel with Sir Robert Hales, the treasurer, and dragged both men out of the building and took them to Tower Green. Their heads were cut off (horribly, it's said that it took eight blows of the axe to behead Simon), then stuck on a pole, paraded to Westminster and finally fixed above Traitors' Gate.

Tyler met Richard again, the next day, and made more demands; but then Tyler was offended by the behaviour of a valet. He tried to stab the man who'd insulted him; when the mayor of London arrested him for violent behaviour, Tyler tried to stab him, too. A fight broke out; Tyler was executed and his head replaced Simon's on the gate.

St Gregory's church Sudbury. Photograph by author.

Simon's body was interred at Canterbury, and his head was brought back to Sudbury. His skull is kept in a special niche in the vestry wall of St Gregory's church; though his teeth were sold off one by one as relics. Kitson says the head was shown as an exhibit as late as 1748 – and that at one point the mouth was open, the skin was tanned and the ears were entire!

It's said that Simon has been seen in the church – and may be responsible for ghostly footsteps heard there.

The Mummified Cat

In the floor of the foyer of the Mill Hotel in Sudbury, there's a mummified cat; it was discovered in 1975 after the mill was converted to a hotel, originally bricked up in the walls to bring good luck. Whenever the cat is removed from the building, it's said that bad luck follows; when the cat was taken away, the person who'd removed it had an accident, there were floods in the manager's office, and problems with the road outside the hotel. The cat was returned, and everything was back to normal.

Mill Hotel, Sudbury. Photograph by author.

It's said that a woman was once killed by being dragged under the wheel when the building was still a mill, and it's believed that her ghost still haunts the older parts of the building.

The Dragon of Sudbury

According to a document in Canterbury Cathedral, two dragons fought on the border between Suffolk and Essex at Ballingdon Hill on 26 September 1449 'at about the hour of Vespers'. The dragon of Suffolk from Kedlington Hill was black, and the dragon of Essex from Ballingdon Hill was red with spots. After a battle that lasted an hour, the red dragon won; however, both dragons survived the fight and returned to their own lairs.

Sutton Hoo

Mound 2 at Sutton Hoo – at its 7th-century level. Photograph by author.

Sutton Hoo (OS grid reference TM 288 487) is a 7th- and early 8th-century barrow cemetery containing two ship burials. The burial from Mound 1 is the best preserved example of North European boat building that has been discovered to date, and has been described as 'page one in the history of Britain'. As well as being the best preserved example from

Mound 1 at Sutton Hoo; the pole in the centre marks where the ship was found. Photograph by author.

141

the period, it's also the largest excavated boat, measuring over 27 metres in length and 4.5 metres in width. In a poll following the 2003 BBC television documentary *Our Top Ten Treasures*, Sutton Hoo ship burial was voted as the third most important treasure unearthed in Britain.

The site is in the care of English Heritage and is open to the public.

The Ghostly Warriors

The story of Sutton Hoo begins with Edith May Pretty, who moved to Sutton Hoo house with her husband in 1926. After his death in 1934, she became interested in spiritualism. Her house overlooks some ancient burial mounds; there were rumours of 'untold gold' in the mounds, and her nephew, who was a dowser, had picked up signals of buried gold.

One evening, she was talking to a friend and looking out of the window at the mounds, when her friend said that she could see ghostly warrior figures walking on the largest mound.

In 1937, she spoke to Ipswich Museum, who put her in touch with their archaeologist, Basil Brown. He went to the site with her; she suggested that he should open the largest mound, now known as Mound 1, but he noted that it had already been disturbed. Instead, in 1938, he opened three smaller mounds – Mounds 2, 3 and 4 – and discovered that the mounds had already been looted. Two of them contained cremation burials, and the third had traces of a buried boat.

The Ghost Ship

The following year, Basil Brown came back to Sutton Hoo. Mrs Pretty persuaded him to open a trench in Mound 1, with the help of her gardener and gamekeeper. He soon discovered iron ship rivets, which he left in place while he continued excavating. Then he realised that he was uncovering the stem of a huge ship. Because the wood had dissolved into the acidic sand that surrounded it, what he was left with was the impression of the ship, like a fossil cast.

The outline of the ship was enormous –27 metres long. Mrs Pretty had been talking to a medium friend, and told Brown to keep digging. He did so, and discovered the burial chamber, where the dead man lay surrounded by his possessions. It was undisturbed – and it was also in the exact spot where Mrs Pretty had suggested that he should dig, the year before.

Excavation in a Hurry

Mrs Pretty contacted the British Museum, and Charles Phillips from Cambridge University took charge of the excavation. The body had not survived in the acidic environment, but there were many treasures, including silver bowls and spoons, armour, weapons and jewellery, along with a leather purse which had a jewelled lid and contained 37 gold coins dating from between 595 and 640, two ingots and three blanks. Many of the items had been damaged by crushing; however, because the war was looming, the archaeologists had to work quickly, recording and removing all the items. A police guard was mounted, but although the work was meant to take place in secret, the story was leaked to the press. The finds were taken to London; there was a treasure trove inquest in August 1939 which decided that Mrs Pretty was the legal owner of the treasure.

The mound was lined with turf and bracken to protect the outline of the ship. The finds were stored safely in the London Underground during the Blitz; and Mrs Pretty, who died in 1942, left the treasures to the nation.

During the war, the site was used as a training ground for tanks and armoured vehicles, but luckily no damage was done to the ship burial. After the war, the British Museum took charge of the research team, and from the mid-1960s Mound 1 was re-excavated and a plaster cast of the ship was taken. The mound was then restored, and the finds were analysed, preserved and reconstructed. Between 1983 and 1992, the site was surveyed again; new burials were discovered, including one of a man and his horse in Mound 3. There was also an undisturbed grave of a man in Mound 17; he had been buried in a coffin with various armour and goods (and some lamb chops!), and a separate grave of a horse lay next to him.

The 'Sandmen'

As well as the Anglo-Saxon graves, there are graves on the site dating from the 9th and 10th centuries. These seem to be the graves of people who had been executed, either by beheading or hanging. The acidic soil had dissolved their bones, so only the impressions of the bodies were left; some were near post holes which suggested that gallows had been raised nearby.

Who Was Buried at Sutton Hoo?

We don't actually know who was buried in the ship, though because he was buried in a large, roofed chamber on the ship he

Replica of the helmet found at Sutton Hoo. Photograph by author.

was very powerful and important. He was buried with objects showing that he had a military authority – including a long sword with a jewelled hilt, spears, an axe and a helmet with a face-mask; the was also a large shield, a whetstone with a stag on top that may have been used as a sceptre, and an iron standard. The fragments of fabrics suggested that he had been buried with a valuable cloak and patterned cloth hangings.

The most likely person is Rædwald, who was the king of the East Angles from about 600 until his death, around 625. He was the first East Anglian ruler to be baptised, although he also kept an altar in his temple to the old pagan gods of his forebears. He became High King of Britain after defeating Æthelfrith, King of Northumbria, at the Battle of the River Idle, around 617.

Walberswick

The journalist Norman Shrapnel called Walberswick 'the spookiest place in England' – and he definitely has a point. Walberswick also has the distinction of having perhaps the most precisely recorded ghost, thanks to George Orwell.

Ruins of the old church at Walberwick. Photograph by author.

The ghost in the churchyard

In 1931, George Orwell was staying in the village. He wrote a letter to his friend Dennis Collings, the son of his family doctor and later a renowned anthropologist, telling him about his experience. He'd been sitting in the ruins of the church – which was originally built in the 1490s but fell into ruins, and in the 1690s the parishioners were given permission to demolish the old church and build a smaller one in the ruins.

He drew a plan of the church and told Collings that 'at about 5.20 p.m. on the 27 July 1931' he was sitting within the ruins [just to the right of the arch in the picture, as you look at it], looking out. He glanced over his shoulder and saw a figure pass through the arch to the left, from inside the ruins to the outside, 'disappearing behind the masonry and presumably emerging into the churchyard.' He wasn't looking directly at the figure so he 'couldn't make out more than that it was a man's figure small & stooping, & dressed in lightish brown ... I had the impression that it glanced towards me in passing, but I made out nothing of the features. At the moment of its passing I thought nothing, but a few seconds later it struck me that the figure had made no noise.'

Naturally, he followed it out into the churchyard 'about 20 seconds after I had seen it', and discovered that there was no-one in the churchyard; although there were two people in the road, they looked nothing like the figure he'd seen. He looked in the church and discovered the vicar, dressed in black (very different from the 'lightish brown' of the man in the churchyard) and a workman who'd been sawing the whole time and was taller than the figure.

Orwell's verdict? 'The figure had therefore vanished, presumably an hallucination.'

Other people have claimed to see the figure in the churchyard and surrounding areas, but his identity is still unknown.

The white dog

Orwell wasn't the only author to have a spooky experience at Southwold. Penelope Fitzgerald said that she was taking a pony across the common when the pony jibbed at something that looked like four large milk bottles. As they drew closer, she saw a white dog like a large pointer, which ran off through the bracken – but the really strange thing was that the dog made no sound at all. On returning to the village, she asked if anyone had reported a similar experience, and was told that the white dog had been waiting for someone on the common for at least 100 years.

The Ghosts of the Ferry

According to the late writer Peter Haining, in the early 20th century a visitor to Walberwick asked Old Todd the ferryman to row him over to Southwold. As he drew near to the small boat, he saw old man holding small child's hand. He sat down; when he realised that Old Todd was going to pull away without the man and child, he said that maybe they ought to wait. But when he looked round,

*The river crossing at Walberswick.
Photograph by author.*

the man and boy had vanished. Old Todd began to row, saying, 'We never wait for them.'

The ghosts were also reported in the 1950s; it's thought that the man and the boy had drowned a couple of hundred years before. Penelope Fitzgerald thought that the ghost at the Walberswick–Southwold crossing was a mother, waiting for her child who was meant to be coming back on the last ferry.

The ghost of the old vicarage

There's a terribly sad tale connected with the Old Vicarage. Until it was destroyed in a World War Two air raid, the Old Vicarage was guest house. A former occupant had many children, but only one of them survived infancy. The mother was so distraught that she killed the child, in case it would suffer or be taken from her. After she died, her ghost was heard crying for her lost children.

The phantom horse

On the common at the Heronry, not far from the Walberswick to Blythburgh road, is a burial mound covered in bracken. On moonlit nights, it's said that a phantom horse emerges from the barrow and gallops over the heath.

Black Shuck

As with much of the coast of Suffolk and Norfolk, Black Shuck has been reported in the area (see page 7 for the story of Shuck). It's probable that smugglers in the area took huge advantage of the tale and embellished it to keep people away from their landing spots (as they did in Norfolk, dressing up a small pony and putting a lantern round its neck to act as the 'glowing eye'). But reports have been made of a black dog, about the size of a calf, which roamed between the vicarage and the Bell Inn.

Another instance occurred outside the Bell Inn some years before, when a coastguard saw something he didn't recognise. He thought it was a smuggler and told him to halt; when the shape continued moving, he fired. Although he was sure he'd hit it, it disappeared without trace…

A story recorded by Morley Adams in 1914, in his book *In the Footsteps of*

The beach at Walberswick. Photograph by author.   *Borrow and Fitzgerald*, tells of an event told by the 'beach-folk' in 'a small seaside hamlet'. He didn't say precisely where the hamlet was; the folklorist Enid Porter places it as 'around Lowestoft', but Walberswick isn't that far down the coast so it could just as well have happened here.

So the story goes, one day a stranger arrived at the hamlet; nobody knew where he came from. Although he was described as 'swarthy' and Italian, he spoke good English. He tried to persuade one of the local fishing boys to go abroad with him, but the boy refused; instead, the stranger asked him to look after a large black dog while he was away. The boy agreed; he continued going for his daily swim, and the dog always joined him.

One particular day, he swam further out to sea than usual – and was horrified to discover that the dog wouldn't let him return to shore. It swam behind him, growling and snapping and driving him further into the sea. The boy was terrified and didn't dare turn to look at the dog – but eventually the dog drew beside him. When the boy looked at him, he saw the Italian man's face rather than the dog's; the man grinned at him in triumph and then turned back into a dog.

The dog sank his teeth into the boy's neck – but when the boy was at the point of going underneath the waves, he managed to hail a passing ship. The crew pulled him aboard; meanwhile, the dog dived into the depths and was never seen again.

The Walberswick Whistle

It's said that sometimes you can hear a whistling sound around Walberswick, which scares animals. Some as that it's the scream of a woman who was once lost in the caves below; others say it it's simply the wind in underground caverns.

Wangford Priory

The Cluniac priory of Wangford (OS grid reference TM 4658 7908) used to be on the south side of the parish church. It was was founded some time before 1160 and dissolved in 1540.

The beginning of the priory

The Cluniac priory was founded as a dependency of Thetford. As with many 'alien' priories during the Hundred Years' War, its property could be seized, but it was possible

Wangford church. Photograph by author.

to buy a letter of denization from the Crown, which would make it a naturalised English monastery. In 1393 the priory was made denizen, on payment of 100 marks (£66 13s 4d, the equivalent of about £32,500 in modern terms). There were between three and five monks at the priory.

Litigation and jail

In 1275, the Hundred jury said that the sheriff, William Giffard, had taken the prior of Wangford, Reginald, violently from the court of Master Philip of Wangford; he then imprisoned the prior in Norwich jail for a week and didn't let him out until he paid an unjust fine of 7 marks (the equivalent of about £780 in modern terms). It isn't recorded whether the prior ever got his money back, or whether Giffard ever had to pay damages.

Clearly there were still tensions between town and gown, because on 23 November 1433 the prior filed a bill in the court of chancery against John Wynde and others, for illegally entering the priory and breaking down the cloister walls.

Dissolution

The monks left the priory in 1537 and the house was leased as a farm; it was finally dissolved, along with Thetford, in 1540, and it was granted to the Duke of Norfolk. Kirby's *Suffolk Traveller,* written in 1735, says that there were substantial ruins attached to the church; the last remaining parts of the priory were demolished in the late 19th century when the church was remodelled. Human remains were found on the site in 1961.

Wingfield Castle

Wingfield Castle (OS grid reference TM 2221 7724) is the remains of a fortified medieval manor house. Only the south curtain wall survives intact, with a gatehouse and polygonal corner bastions. The present house, dating from the mid-16th century, was built into the remains of the western curtain wall. It is on private land and there is no access to the public.

Wingfield castle. Photograph by author.

The beginnings of the castle

The license to crenellate (fortify) the house was granted by Richard II in 1382 to Michael de la Pole, who became Lord Chancellor of England in 1383 and Earl of Suffolk in 1385 (though Parliament was critical of the way the king – and de la Pole – handled the country's finances). He married Catherine, the daughter of Sir John Wingfield, who had been the Black Prince's chief counsellor; Michael built the castle at Wingfield on the site of an earlier manor house.

In 1387, Parliament demanded the removal of Michael – he was one of Richard II's four personal advisors and Parliament saw him as an obstacle. The king

Remains of Wingfield Castle; plate from Thomas Kitson Cromwell's Excursions Through Suffolk, *1818-9. Photograph by author.*

refused, saying, 'I will not dismiss one of my scullions at Parliament's command.' Michael was impeached on seven charges related to his chancellorship. The big three were that he hadn't implemented the reforms agreed, hadn't made sure that the tax grated by parliament had been spent on the navy as agreed, and didn't send help to the rebels in Ghent, so it was lost to Burgundy. Suffolk successfully argued that these failings were not his alone. However, he wasn't able to defend himself against four charges of misusing his position to further his interests, and was sentenced to forfeit lands held by royal grant and income from an annuity he'd misappropriated. He was thrown into jail until he'd paid a fine of 20,000 marks (£13,333 6s. 8d. – equivalent to about £4.8 million in modern terms). However, by Christmas he was free to join the king at Windsor – and spent the next year widening the rift between the king and his opponents. On 14 November Gloucester, Arundel and Warwick appealed him and four close associates on a charge of treason. Suffolk fled abroad, disguised as a Flemish poulterer, and tried to get refuge in Calais where his brother Edmund was captain of the castle – but Edmund refused to do it without the permission of the town governor, who sent Michael back to London.

Suffolk managed to escape to Paris, but was convicted in his absence of accroaching the royal power, trying to impede the work of the commission established in the previous parliament, and using his influence over the king to further his own ends. He was sentenced to death, but died in exile in Paris in 1389.

Wooden effigy of Michael de la Pole resting on the head of his enemy, Wingfield church. Photograph by author.

Wooden effigy of Michael de la Pole and his wife, Wingfield church. Photograph by author.

Michael's son – also called Michael – succeeded him and was restored to the de la Pole lands and title as the second Earl of Suffolk. He went to France with Henry V in 1415 and died of dysentery at the siege of Harfleur; his body was shipped home and he was buried in Wingfield church, where his wooden effigy lies.

Michael's son – yet another Michael – was the third Earl of Suffolk; however, he only lasted for a couple of weeks because he was killed at the battle of Agincourt. The English chroniclers described him 'as strong, as active and as daring as any member of the court'.

The beheading of William de la Pole

William, the second son of the second Earl, succeeded as the fourth Earl at the age of 19 after his brother's death. He'd been involved in the wars against the French, being seriously wounded at the siege of Harfleur, and became the joint commander of the British forces at Orleans. When he was completely surrounded in June 1429, he said he would only surrender to Joan of Arc – 'the bravest woman on earth' and allegedly wanted to knight her. He said later that his ransom was £20,000 (the equivalent of just over £4 million in modern terms), but he was released early in 1430.

He became an ally of Cardinal Beaufort and negotiated the marriage treaty between the king and Margaret of Anjou. Once the terms were agreed, the king sent him to bring her back to England, and created him Marquis of Suffolk.

After the deaths of Beaufort and Humphrey of Gloucester (and many people believed that Suffolk had conspired to murder him – see page 34), he became the main power behind the throne. Henry VI made him Lord Chamberlain, Lord High Admiral of England, and finally Duke of Suffolk in 1448.

However, England then lost many territories in the north of France – this wasn't helped by the unfavourable terms of the marriage treaty, which included a secret clause to give Normandy back to France. He was arrested on 28 January 1450 and thrown into the Tower of London. Parliament accused him of treason; The king, trying to screen his favourite and also stop damaging details of government leaking out, banished him for five years. However, William was intercepted at Dover – possibly arranged by the Duke of York, his enemy – given a mock trial, and beheaded on a ship 'in the name of the community of the realm' before his body was thrown into the sea. He was found near Dover, and his body was brought back for burial at Wingfield.

John de la Pole

John de la Pole, Willam's son, married Lady Margaret Beaufort in 1450 (when she was 7 and he was 8), though Henry VI annulled the marriage in 1453 so Edmund Tudor could marry her. Although the Duke of York had been his father's enemy, John supported York in the Wars of the Roses. He married Elizabeth Neville –

Alabaster effigy of John de la Pole resting on the head of his Saracen enemy, Wingfield church. Photograph by author.

Alabaster effigy of John de la Pole and wife Elizabeth, Wingfield church. Photograph by author.

Edward IV and Richard III's sister. When Michael had been executed in 1450, the Dukedom had become forfeit; Edward IV restored the title by letters patent, and John became the second Duke of Suffolk in 1463.

After Bosworth, he submitted to Henry VII and served him loyally; he died in 1491/2 and was buried in Wingfield.

The Rebel Duke

John de la Pole (son of the John above) was made the 1st Earl of Lincoln and was designated the heir to the throne for Richard III. Although he submitted to Henry VII after Bosworth, he supported the claims of Lambert Simnel to the crown – Lambert was a pretender who claimed to be the Earl of Warwick, Edward IV's nephew. However, Henry VII produced Warwick from the tower in 1487 to prove that it was a lie, and offered to pardon the offenders if they submitted. John fled to Burgundy and was attainted as a traitor. He joined a rebellion against Henry VII, but was killed at the battle of Stoke Field in 1487.

Edmund de la Pole, the Earl of Lincoln's brother (John's third son), gave up his claim to a dukedom in exchange for the return of the lands forfeited by the Earl of Lincoln. He spent much of his time in financial difficulties, and ended up fleeing abroad in 1499. He was brought back, and had to pay a huge fine; he went into exile again in 1501, and was outlawed by the king in 1502. Although he was given a promise that his life would be spared, when he returned to the country in 1506 he was thrown into the Tower of London and not pardoned at Henry VIII's accession. When his brother Richard was recognised as the King of England by Louis XII of France (on the grounds of his Yorkist bloodline), Henry VIII executed him.

The castle passed to Edmund's brother Richard, who died in 1525; then the house went to the Catelyn family, who built the Tudor farmhouse in about 1544. The drawbridge to the castle was removed in 1750 and a bridge was put in its place.

The Green Children of Woolpit

St Mary's church, Woolpit. Photograph by author.

The manor of Woolpit once belonged to the abbey of Bury St Edmunds. One of the strangest stories in Suffolk is about the green children of Woolpit, which is said to have taken place during the reign of King Stephen – although there is no mention of it in the Anglo-Saxon Chronicles, which deals with English history up to Stephen's death in 1154.

There are two main sources of the story; one is by William of Newburgh in his *Historia rerum Anglicarum* (*History of English Affairs*), which tells the history of England from 1066 to 1198. The other is by Ralph of Coggeshall, who was the sixth abbot of Coggeshall Abbey in Essex, in his *Chronicles*.

So the story goes, one day, while the men of Woolpit were working in the fields, they heard cries for help coming from one of the pits that had been dug to trap wolves. They discovered two children, a boy and a girl; they spoke in a strange tongue, and nobody could understand a word they said. Their clothes were of an unfamiliar design and made from a material that nobody recognised. But, strangest of all, the children's skin was green.

Village sign showing the green children, Woolpit. Photograph by author.

The villagers helped them out of the pit and took them to the house of the lord of the manor, Sir Richard de Calne, a few miles away at Wikes. Richard couldn't get any sense out of them either, and the children were tearful and refused to eat any food brought to them. The boy in particular was quite ill, and the villagers were worried that he might die; however, then some beans were brought in from the field with the stalks still attached. The children fell on them, but instead of opening the pods they tried to open the stalks. When they discovered that the stalks were empty, they wept even harder.

Then someone showed them how to open the pods; they immediately ate the beans. Thinking that maybe the children liked the colour of the food, as it was the same colour as their skins, the villagers offered them other green vegetables, which they ate with alacrity.

Over time, the boy sickened and eventually died; however, the girl learned to speak English and to eat normal food. She then told the story of how she ended up at Woolpit. She said that they came from a place called St Martin's Land; it was perpetual twilight in her land, and the people all had green skin. She wasn't quite sure where St Martin's Land was, but there was a wide river separating it from another land, which looked luminous. One day, she and her brother had been

156

looking after her father's herds and had followed them into a cavern. They became lost, then heard the sound of bells and followed the noise, which led them to the bottom of the pit where they had been found.

When she grew up, she became de Calne's servant and apparently married a merchant from Kings Lynn (though other sources say that she married a man from Lavenham). Some accounts say that she took the name Agnes Barre. The story has been repeated over the years, in Robert Burton's *The Anatomy of Melancholy* (1621) and Thomas Keightley's *The Fairy Mythology* (1828).

So how true is the story? Both 12th-century accounts were written quite a while after the event, although Ralph of Coggeshall said that he got the story from Richard de Calne. There is no historical record of a Richard de Calne, although there is a Wakes Colne Manor in Essex; it's possible that there were transcription errors when the story was originally written down.

The most widely accepted explanation is that of Paul Harris, written in *Fortean Studies 4* (1998). He thinks that the date of the story is wrong, and it took place during the reign of Henry II; in 1173, there was a huge battle between Henry's supporters and the Flemish mercenaries at nearby Fornham (see page 92). Harris's theory is that the children had lived at Fornham St Martin, near the River Lark, and when their parents were killed they escaped into Thetford Forest. Because they were starving and wandering in the dark forest, their skin had turned green; and because they were Flemish their clothes would have been of a different style to English clothes. He also thinks that the children are heard the sound of bells from Bury St Edmunds, ended up in the mine workings at Grimes Graves, and followed a tunnel through to Woolpit.

However, this explanation has a few holes. For a start, landowners would either have fought on the side of the king or with Bigod and the mercenaries, son Richard would have come across Flemish people before and would have recognised the children's accents, even if he didn't understand what they were saying. It's also unlikely that the children would have been able to hear the bells from that far away; and the mines are limited to one area, without any connecting passages to Woolpit. Given that the children were starving, would they have had the strength to walk a distance of nearly 20 miles?

The fairies of Stowmarket

Woolpit isn't the only place where fairies have been seen; Southwold (see page 136) has the 'fairy hills', and Stowmarket has its 'farisees' or 'ferishers'.

In 1842, the Rev A. G. H. Hollingsworth was given an account of a sighting of fairies, 20 years before, by a man who lived at the cottages by the hop ground. The man was coming back to Stowmarket from Bury when he saw a dozen fairies in a field, wearing sparkling dresses 'with spangles like the girls at shows at Stow fair', holding hands and moving in a circle. He said he was perfectly sober at the time, and about 40 yards away from them; he couldn't make out their faces, but the tallest was 3 feet high and the smallest was the size of a doll. He described them as 'light and shadowy, not like solid bodies', and he went by, saying 'Lord have mercy on me, but them must be the fairies'. When he got home, he persuaded three women to go back with him and see them, but the fairies had disappeared.

Another elderly resident told Hollingsworth that a hundred years before, fairies had visited houses in Tavern Street; as the fairies never appeared when anyone was nearby, people hid and waited to see them. They disappeared as soon as they realised someone was there – and allegedly, when people walked upstairs in a house after disturbing them, 'sparks of fire as bright as stars' appeared under their feet.

And yet another elderly resident told Hollingsworth that either she or her sister had almost become a changeling; one night, soon after the birth, her mother 'missed the babe' and was worried that the fairies had taken her. She jumped out of bed and saw the baby at the foot of the bed. The fairies were undressing the child; when they saw the mother, they disappeared in a hole in the floor. Apparently, for months afterwards, the woman slept with the baby safely between herself and her husband and pinned its clothes to the pillow and sheets so it wouldn't be taken by the fairies.

Selected bibliography

Walter Henry Barrett, *East Anglian Folklore and Other Tales*, London, Routlege & Kegan Paul, 1976, ISBN 0710083009

Mel Birch, *Suffolk's Ancient Sites – Historic Places*, Castell Publishing, Mendlesham 2004, ISBN 094813450X

Thomas Kitson Cromwell, *Excursions Through Suffolk*, 2 volumes, London 1818-9

William Dugdale, *Monasticon Anglicanum*, 1817

Peter Haining, *The Supernatural Coast*, Robert Hale 1992, ISBN 0709047223

M. R. James, *Suffolk and Norfolk – A perambulation of the two counties with notices of their history and their ancient buildings*, JM Dent, London 1930

Robert Malster, *A History of Ipswich*, Phillimore & Co, Chichester 2000, ISBN 1860771483

Frank Meeres, *A History of Bury St Edmunds*, Phillimore & Co, Chichester 2002, ISBN 1860772277

Alan Murdie, *Haunted Bury St Edmunds*, Tempus, Stroud 2006, ISBN 075242404X

William Page (ed), *A History of the County of Suffolk Volume 2*, Victoria County History 1907

Enid Porter, *The Folklore of East Anglia*, B. T. Batsford Ltd, London 1974, ISBN 0713427930

Granville Squiers, *Secret Hiding Places*, London, Stanley Paul, 1934

Alfred Inigo Suckling, *The History and Antiquities of the County of Suffolk*, London 1848

Peter Tryon, *The Castles of Suffolk*, Poppyland, Cromer 2004. ISBN 0946148686

Jennifer Westwood and Jacqueline Simpson, *The Lore of the Land*, Penguin, London 2005, ISBN 9780141007113

Archive copies of the *Ipswich Journal*